ATLANTA

The Right Kind of Courage

© BILLY HOWARD

URBAN TAPESTRY SERIES

TOWERY
PUBLISHING, INC.

ATLA

NTA

The Right Kind of Courage

Introduction by
President Jimmy Carter

Art Direction by
Jil Foutch

4

Contents

▼ © BUD LEE

WHEN I WAS GROWING UP ON A PEANUT FARM IN PLAINS DURING the Great Depression, I saw Atlanta as an exciting, mysterious place. It was exhilarating for me to travel with my father and uncle from our small town of a few hundred people to the big city 130 miles north, where they sold mules and shopped wholesale for our mercantile supplies. I recall standing in awe at the order counter in the huge Sears, Roebuck building and crossing Ponce de Leon, to cheer for the Atlanta Crackers baseball team.

I later visited Atlanta with my high school class, touring places such as the capitol and the Cyclorama. However, it wasn't until college that I spent more time in the city. After my freshman year at Georgia Southwestern College in Americus, I transferred to Georgia Tech, where I lived in the dormitory adjacent to Tech Stadium. Having no car, I walked or rode the streetcar. I sometimes ventured downtown, but mostly lived the monastic life of a student.

Time passed, routing me to my first of two terms in the state senate in 1962. Rather than establishing a home in the capital, I stayed in the old Henry Grady Hotel. I usually left our family car in Plains for my wife, Rosalynn, who was caring for our three children and couldn't accompany me to Atlanta very often. So I walked every day from downtown to the capitol, gaining "sidewalk" insight about the community—something I recommend to anyone who really wants to explore a big city. The people, the buildings, the perspective—all become very personal when you're on foot.

© RICHARD CUMMINS / PHOTOPHILE

During the 1960s, Atlanta was seen as the beacon of racial enlightenment throughout the Southeast. The guiding influence of the *Atlanta Journal-Constitution*, Ralph McGill, and some fine mayors such as Ivan

Allen Jr. helped Atlanta send a clear signal throughout Georgia—and throughout the South—that we should overcome the devastating effects of both legal and practical racial segregation.

And it was in this decade that the state senate began considering legislation that acquainted me more with Atlanta's poverty and racial segregation. I began to realize there were two Atlantas—the one where the decision makers lived in decent homes, with good jobs and access to good schools, and the other in low-income areas, where people often lacked medical care and sound education or even basic necessities such as food and shelter. This realization continued to grow throughout my tenure as governor, which began in 1971, and marked the only period that I lived full-time in Atlanta.

After serving as president, I returned to Plains to farm and see how I might continue to foster human rights, peace, democracy, and freedom. Rosalynn and I decided to create a nonprofit, politically neutral institution that could cut through governmental barriers or bureaucratic red tape and tackle, directly and forthrightly, the causes of personal suffering.

Several universities nationwide offered us teaching positions and the opportunity to establish a center for peace, but we wanted to stay in Georgia. Atlanta is home to many fine colleges and universities, and

we were pleased to accept an offer to become part of the Emory University community. So with the help of many like-minded individuals, we established The Carter Center in one room of the Emory library in late 1982.

I joined the faculty as a distinguished professor, lecturing in all schools and colleges of the university, which I continue to do today. Rosalynn became a distinguished fellow at Emory's Institute for Women's Studies, where she joins with other prominent women to discuss national and international issues.

Our Center started with just a few employees, but with many big ideas and dreams. By 1985, we had raised enough money to start building The Carter Center, along with the Presidential Library and Museum, between the Emory campus and downtown Atlanta. (We later donated the Library and Museum to the federal government, which operates it under the auspices of the National Archives.) Legend has it that our location, on Copenhill, is where General William Tecumseh Sherman watched Atlanta burn during the Civil War. Rosalynn and I are pleased that it is now a place from which we can contribute to the city's building and further development—socially, economically, and intellectually.

Although Plains is still home, we stay a week or so every month in our small apartment at the Center. With so many ties to Atlanta, it's

hard not to feel that we also belong here. I often stand at our apartment's window, which overlooks 35 acres of rolling hills, gardens, and lakes, and marvel at the spectacular skyline. This city truly has come into its own.

But amid the splendor, unprecedented prosperity, and growth, we realized upon our return in the mid-1980s that Atlanta still suffered from devastating social ills, like most major urban centers in this country. These included many issues we wanted to address as private citizens—poverty, racial injustice, the drug culture, high infant mortality rates, and limited access to basic services.

From its inception, The Carter Center was dedicated to advancing peace and health worldwide, and our work is conducted on many levels. We have negotiated cease-fires in places such as Bosnia, Haiti, and Sudan, and have monitored and mediated critical elections in emerging democracies in Africa and Latin America. In some of these same nations, we have programs that prevent devastating diseases and teach farmers to increase crop production. Rather than give handouts, create large bureaucracies, or duplicate other organizations' efforts, Center staff provide people with the tools and knowledge to make changes in their own lives.

During its first decade, The Carter Center worked mostly in other countries. But all the while, I sensed there would be no better place to practice The Carter Center's mission than right in our own backyard. In many ways, the suffering in Atlanta's poor communities was every bit as intense as what the Center encountered in impoverished or war-torn countries.

So, in 1992, Rosalynn and I initiated The Atlanta Project, or TAP, a program that has helped bridge the divide between the two Atlantas— rich and poor.

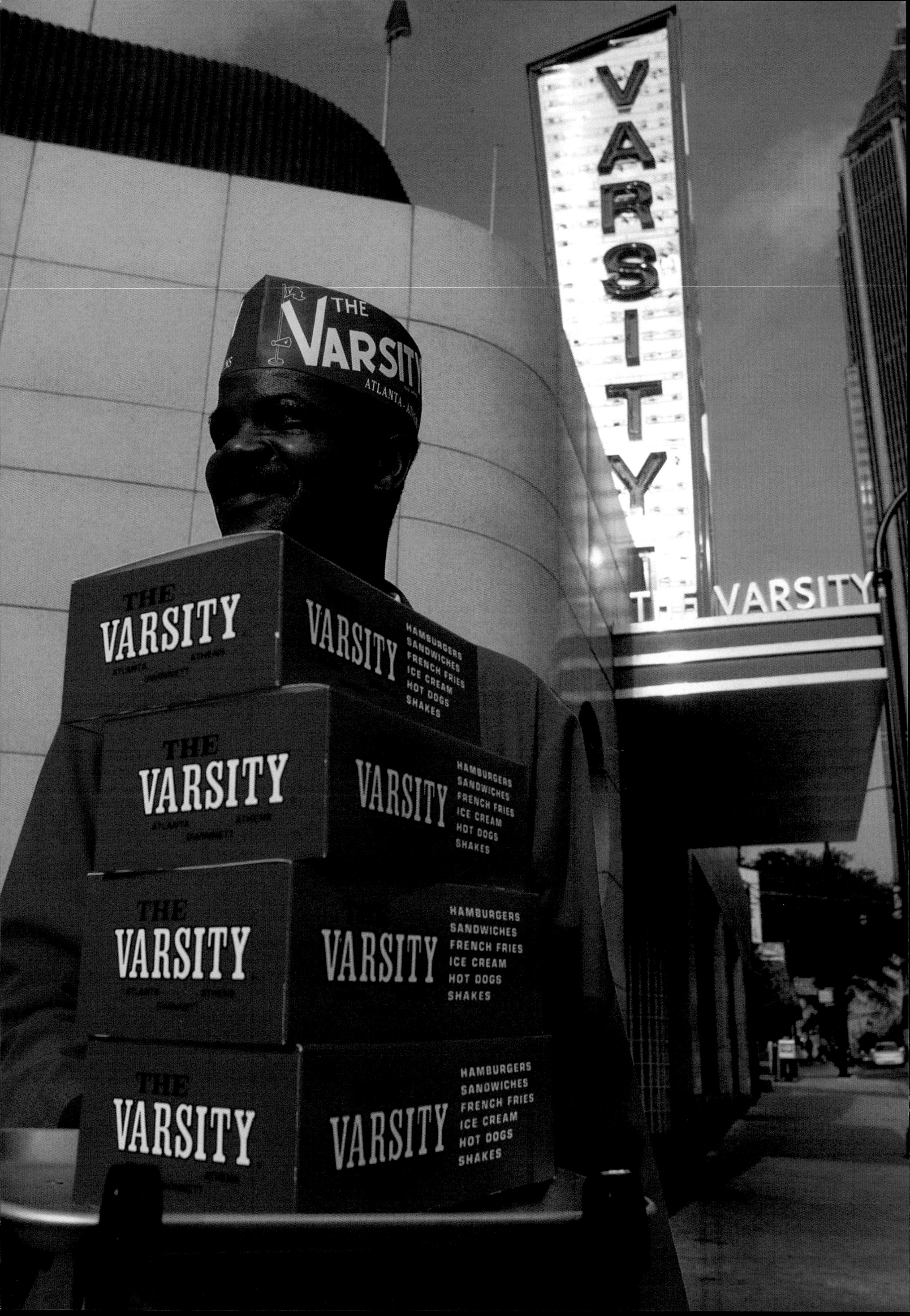

We began TAP by focusing on 20 neighborhoods in the city's neediest areas. We asked residents how we could help, and gave them the opportunity to invite us into their lives. Next, we induced corporations to form individual partnerships with these communities and to work closely with the residents to find lasting improvements to major problems that they identified. Corporations didn't merely write checks; they assigned top-level executives to staff community offices and work alongside neighborhood residents. We trained volunteers. We explored ways to improve poor housing, reduce crime, provide avenues for health care, and help people gain useful skills to find good jobs. And, we opened lines of communication and established bonds of trust between groups of people—the two Atlantas—who lived in separate worlds.

Among those participating were many of the major international and national corporations that have a presence in Atlanta, as well as a number of local companies. These businesses and others have become more aware of the vast economic divisions in Atlanta and have embraced a new perception of the city. They have proved that besides making a profit, they can make a difference. Following their example, almost two dozen of the city's major institutions of higher learning, including public and private universities and colleges, also partnered with The Atlanta Project communities to share their knowledge and

provide educational opportunities. It also took courage from city and government leaders and all facets of the Atlanta community to focus so publicly on the city's problems.

When Atlanta was booming economically, TAP helped strengthen the city's all-important sense of community. TAP opened the door to building organizational and interpersonal connections that did not exist: between corporations and low-income neighborhoods, between and among people of different races and backgrounds, and between previously isolated segments of our community and people they never would have met otherwise. As a result, many of our neediest citizens have found new hope and greater confidence in their ability to affect the future.

In keeping with The Carter Center's overseas policies, we planned to limit TAP to five years, encouraging people to be independent and find ways to help themselves. During this time, many of those 20 communities, in effect, graduated from us, while others required more help. So we extended TAP for three years to the fall of 1999. However, some of the community partnerships with corporations and educational institutions will continue, and we believe many program benefits will be

permanent. While no one answer can "cure" society's ills, Atlanta has decided that the only real failure is to stop trying.

As I travel throughout the world, people frequently ask me to speak about The Atlanta Project—about what we have learned from our successes and failures. Interest has been so consistently high that The America Project was created in 1994 to convey our message to other cities that are struggling as we are to address poverty, racial polarization, and the growing alienation between the haves and the have-nots. In the past several years, The America Project has shared TAP's experiences with leaders from more than 300 communities.

Today, Atlanta has vitality and influence, and is prospering socially and economically. For example, several years ago, UPS moved its corporate headquarters here, joining such giants as Coca-Cola and contributing to unprecedented corporate growth. The success of the universities here also has been outstanding. All of these things have been a credit and benefit to the people of Atlanta, the state of Georgia, and the entire region.

Also adding to our quality of life are our world-famous Braves and up-and-coming Falcons. Our major sports teams' successes have raised our collective spirit and helped introduce Atlanta to the rest of the country.

K EEPING THE CITY OF ATLANTA on the minds of many is the job of civic leaders such as Mayor Bill Campbell (OPPOSITE) and Atlanta Convention and Visitors Bureau President Spurgeon Richardson.

R EFLECTING THE GROWTH of a modern city on the rise, Atlanta has built a skyline of dynamic proportions (PAGES 28-33).

A T L A N T A

THE RIGHT KIND OF COURAGE

ATLANTA

R EMNANTS OF AN EARLIER TIME, the hotels of old Atlanta now serve as low-rent apartment complexes, or—in the case of the Frances Hotel (TOP LEFT)—have been demolished to make way for newer buildings.

© RICHARD CUMMINS / PHOTOPHILE

FROM DEPICTIONS OF THE COMmon man in Underground Atlanta (BOTTOM) to the frolicking female nudes of John Portman's *Ballet Olympia* (OPPOSITE), public sculpture abounds in the city. Artist Peter Calaboyais, of Greek descent, created *Tribute* (TOP RIGHT) in Centennial Olympic Park in homage to the origin of the Olympics in Athens. After creating a statue of Southern Railway's first president, Samuel Spencer (TOP LEFT), sculptor Daniel C. French went on to make the Lincoln Memorial.

THE RIGHT KIND OF COURAGE

UNDERGROUND ATLANTA—A 12-block area filled with stores, restaurants, and bars—got its name from a decision to raise people and traffic above the congestion of downtown railroad tracks by building a series of concrete viaducts overhead. Left with little choice, store owners followed suit, moving operations up and deserting what had once been their street-level storefronts. The vacated "underground" space was ultimately converted to a tourist site.

O PENED IN 1928 AND LISTED on Atlanta's registry of historic buildings, the Varsity (ABOVE LEFT) sells more Coca-Cola than any other single outlet in the up two miles of hot dogs a day. With just as much grease, but less fanfare, Majestic Food Shops (OPPOSITE) has tempted Emory University students with pleasing a restaurant by its neon, for the Buckhead Diner (ABOVE RIGHT) is a modern, upscale establishment— pretending to be a greasy spoon.

ATLANTA

TURN RIGHT AT THE BIG, RED chicken. Navigating your way through Atlanta's city streets can be an experience fraught with peril. Fortunately, a few well-placed, whimsical landmarks provide for precise directions.

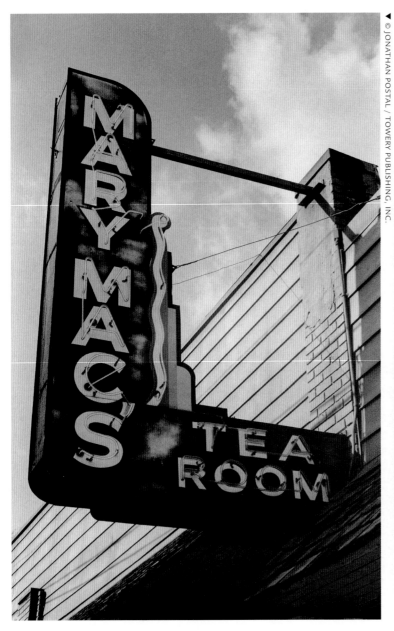

PATRONS OF MARY MAC'S TEA Room have reason to smile. Since 1945, despite a series of ownership changes, the spot has remained a fixture on the Atlanta scene.

TOASTING THE TOWN COMES easy to Robert Jones (ABOVE), who until mid-1999 was the renowned wine steward for the Dining Room at Ritz-Carlton Buckhead. Just prior to his departure for grapier pastures, Jones was chosen by *Food & Wine* as the city's best sommelier. Equally acclaimed for his many acting and directing roles in the Atlanta theater community, Stuart Culpepper (OPPOSITE) knows how to raise a glass to his city as well.

ONE MAN WHO REALLY KNOWS how to please the palates of epicureans is Guenter Seeger, whose restaurant, Seeger's, joins only 17 others as a recipient of the Five-Star Award from *Mobil Travel* *Guide*. Before opening his own place, Seeger was chef for the Dining Room at the Ritz-Carlton Buckhead, the city's only other five-star restaurant.

F ROM THE ITALIAN FARES OF Dominick's (TOP LEFT) and Salvatore Trattoria (TOP RIGHT) to the Mediterranean cuisine of Basil's in Buckhead (BOTTOM LEFT) to the Atlanta Brewing Co.'s Red Brick Ale (BOTTOM RIGHT), Atlanta's culinary scene can delight the most discriminating of taste buds.

54

As Chef Jamie Adams (OPPOSITE) of Veni Vidi Vici knows, fresh produce is invaluable, and locals can often be found perusing the aisles of the DeKalb Farmers Market (TOP), the Sweet Auburn Curb Market (BOTTOM), or the State Farmers Market (PAGES 56 AND 57) in order to find the best harvest.

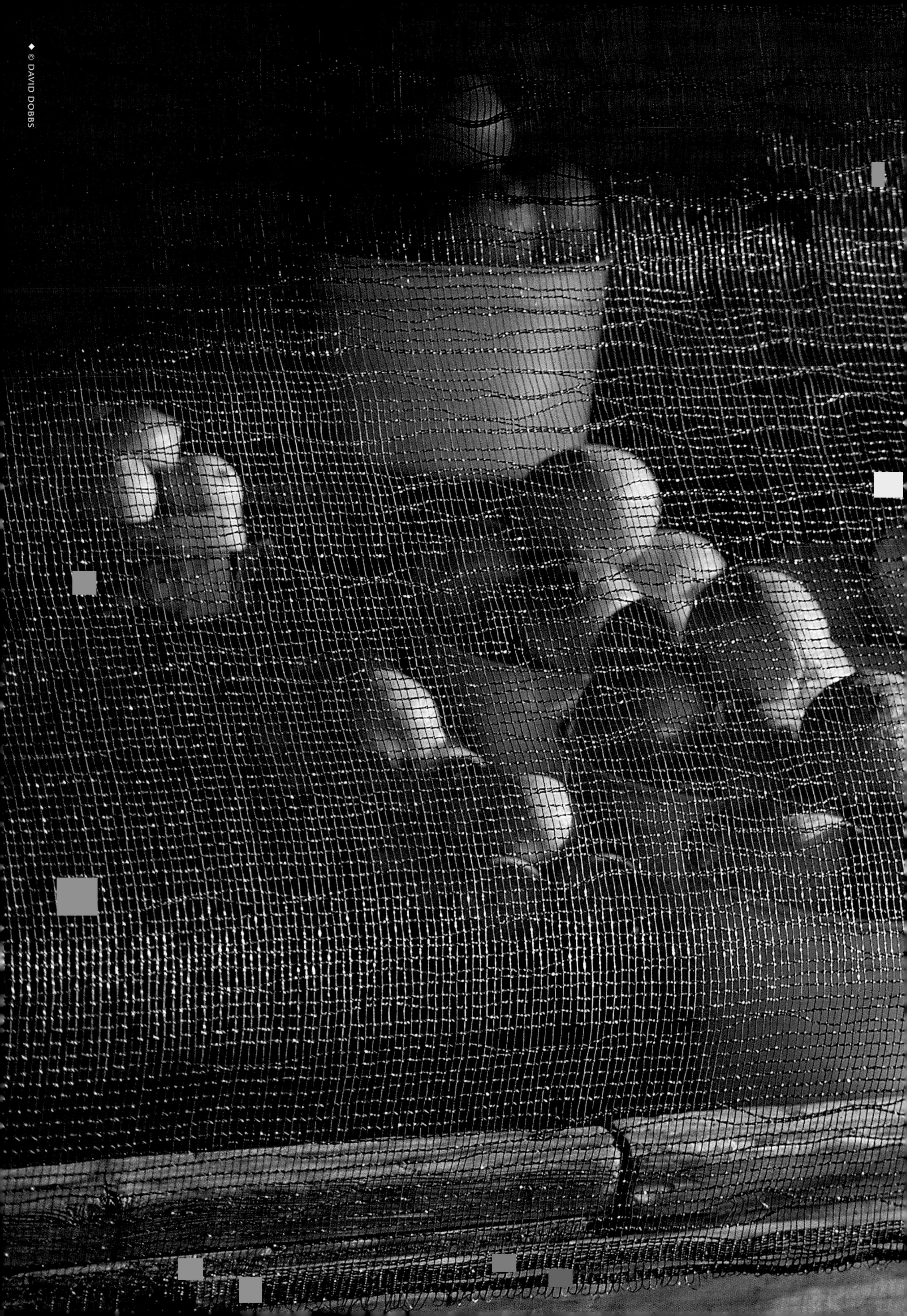

© DAVID DOBBS

THE DOROTHY CHAPMAN FUQUA Conservatory, on the grounds of the Atlanta Botanical Garden, is a $5.5 million glasshouse that is home to a variety of exotic plants. Special rooms showcase rare foliage from all over the world, and three large terrariums are home to an exhibit of brilliantly colored poison dart frogs.

THE ATLANTA BOTANICAL Garden, situated on 30 acres within Piedmont Park, offers quiet moments in the midst of lush landscaping.

ATLANTA

© NIGEL MARSON

THE SWEEPING JAPANESE garden of the Carter Center (OPPOSITE) shows Atlanta at its finest. Helping to keep the city's residential gardens looking professional in their own right, *Atlanta Journal-Constitution* gardening columnist Lee May holds the key to happy horticulture in his hands.

REPRESENTING THE POPULAR Gothic-Tudor style of the 1920s, Lullwater House (ABOVE) and Callanwolde (OPPOSITE) were originally owned by the sons of Coca-Cola Company founder Asa G. Candler. Though no longer inhabited by the first family of soft drink, the beautiful homes have not been forgotten. Lullwater House now serves as home to Emory University's president, and Callanwolde is a fine arts center.

ATLANTA

ONCE ONE OF ATLANTA'S grand old streets lined with multifamily complexes and apartments, Ponce de Leon Avenue has seen some changes over the years. Today, Ponce Manor (ABOVE) serves as a personal-care home, while historic Ponce de Leon Apartments (OPPOSITE) maintains its hold on luxurious housing in the form of condominiums. Opened in 1913, the Beaux Arts and Renaissance Revival building forms one part of a trio of famous sites—which also includes the Georgian Terrace and Fox Theatre—at the intersection of Ponce de Leon Avenue and Peachtree Street.

CABBAGETOWN, ADJACENT TO the nine-building Fulton Bag and Cotton Mill complex, was built in the 1880s to provide homes for mill workers. Consisting of 18 blocks of shotgun cottages, the development has experienced a renewal since the mill's closing in 1977.

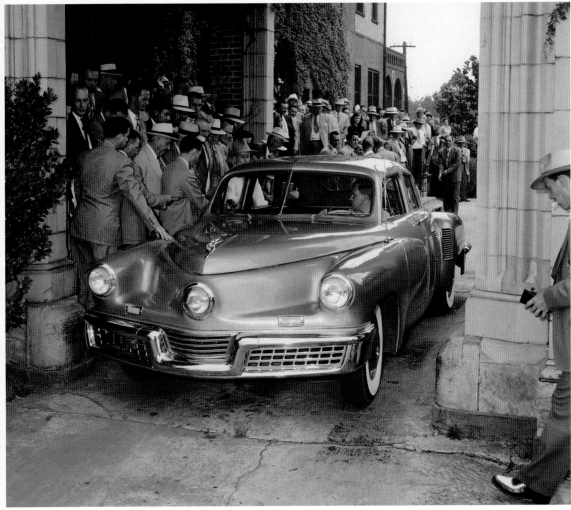

T HE OLD LAKEWOOD SPEEDWAY
was once known as the Grand
Old Lady of Racing, back in
the days when little-known winners
such as Paul Smith (OPPOSITE TOP)
sped around the track. These days,
stock car racing is one of the largest
spectator sports in the nation, and
fans flock to the Atlanta Motor
Speedway to see champions such
as wunderkind Jeff Gordon (TOP).

I N 1996, ATLANTA WAS HOST to the Centennial Olympic Games, welcoming 11,000 athletes from 197 nations. Though the games were marked by stifling heat—the city is not idly called Hotlanta—and a deadly pipe bomb planted in Centennial Olympic Park, the spirit of the competitors and the spectators did not bow. And in the end, the strength and skill of the athletes were the attributes etched in common memory, from the first Irishwoman to win a gold medal to the courageous vault by injured gymnast Kerri Strug.

© ROD KAYE

A TLANTA'S SPORTS ARENAS ARE arguably some of the best in the business. Originally known as Olympic Stadium, the entertainment complex now called Turner Field (OPPOSITE TOP) is home to the Atlanta Braves. The NFL's Atlanta Falcons play in the Georgia Dome (THIS PAGE), a multi-purpose facility that can expand to seat 80,000 spectators underneath its cable-supported dome.

ATLANTA

BEHIND THE BATS OF SUCH greats as Hank Aaron and Chipper Jones (OPPOSITE BOTTOM) and the pitching prowess of John Smoltz (LEFT), the Atlanta Braves have risen to become one of the preeminent teams in baseball. Owned by Ted Turner (OPPOSITE, TOP LEFT) and managed by Bobby Cox (OPPOSITE, TOP RIGHT), the Braves hold the distinction of being the oldest continuously operating professional sports franchise in America.

SOME OF THE BIGGEST NAMES in Georgia sports are—hands down—the men behind the scenes of the Atlanta Braves and Turner Field, including (BOTTOM, FROM LEFT) owner Ted Turner, chairman of the board of directors William Bartholomay, Turner Broadcasting CEO Terence McGuirk, Braves President Stan Kasten, and General Manager John Schuerholz. In addition to his role as center for the Atlanta Hawks, Dikembe Mutombo (OPPOSITE) has been generating a bit of name recognition himself off the court as one of a handful of celebrities starring in Charles Schwab's "SmarterInvestors" series of television commercials. But say good-bye to Georgia Tech's Stephon Marbury (TOP RIGHT) and Coach Bobby Cremins (TOP LEFT). Marbury moved on to the NBA, and Cremins resigned, effective the end of the 1999-2000 season.

ALTHOUGH WE CAN'T ALL be superstars like Andre Agassi (TOP LEFT)—a past winner of Atlanta's AT&T Tennis Challenge—everyone has a little star athlete inside.

ATLANTA'S RECREATIONAL
sports scene is soaring.
From shooting some hoops
in a local park to the new water
sport wakeboarding, the Atlanta
area provides an arena for almost
any kind of entertainment.

I N 1926, A POPULAR COLUMNIST at the *Atlanta Journal* began writing a book that would forever change the way the world viewed Atlanta and the South. Called *Gone With the Wind*, the book remains the best-selling novel of all time, and Margaret Mitchell's tombstone in Oakland Cemetery still attracts droves of admirers.

F RANKLIN GARRETT'S ROLE AS
Atlanta's designated historian
represented a respectful nod
to his factual prowess, even though
it wasn't an officially sanctioned
position. Prior to his death at 93
in early 2000, Garrett (OPPOSITE)
served as the source for the city's
past, writing its definitive story in
*Atlanta and Environs: A Chronicle
of Its People and Events*. Keeping
a truly classic piece of the city's
memories alive, Mary Rose Taylor
(ABOVE), executive director of
the Margaret Mitchell House and
Museum, oversees the famous
writer's home as well as a collection of artifacts from the movie
version of Mitchell's famous novel,
Gone With the Wind.

IN 1966, THE ATLANTA HIS-
torical Society acquired cotton
broker Edward Inman's 25-
acre estate. The society used the
house and grounds to create the
comprehensive and educational
Atlanta History Center, featuring
the 83,000-square-foot Atlanta
History Museum. Inman's 1928
mansion, Swan House (OPPOSITE),
came complete with most of the
original furnishings, and today
serves as a reminder of Old South
wealth.

VISITORS TO THE ATLANTA History Center can get a sense of rural southern life from the Tullie Smith Farm. With the main house—built east of Atlanta in 1845 and moved to the center some 130 years later— listed on the National Register of Historic Places, this site features tours conducted by period-costumed interpreters.

ISTORIC WATERS RUN DEEP in the South, and old covered bridges—such as the Civil War-era Concord Road bridge (OPPOSITE) and the Stone Mountain grist mill bridge (LEFT)—offer a picturesque view of a sometimes turbulent past.

AKING 300 MILLION YEARS to emerge in its present state, Stone Mountain is the world's largest exposed mass of granite. The bas-relief carving— also the world's largest—on the mountain's north side features (BOTTOM, FROM LEFT) Confederate President Jefferson Davis, as well as Generals Robert E. Lee and Stonewall Jackson.

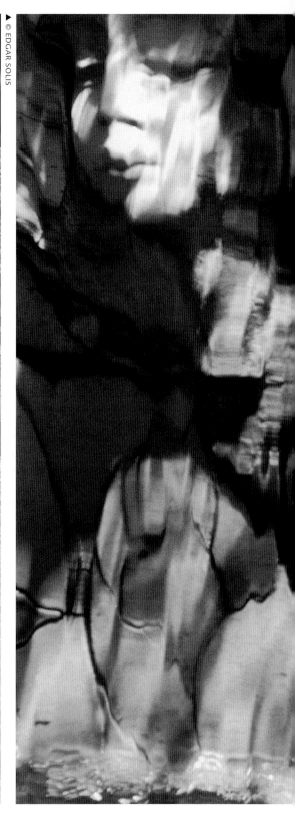

ATLANTA

O FTEN IT'S THE SHADOWS
and subtle touches of a city
that most define and point
to its true character.

A T L A N T A

PHOTOGRAPHY CORSON DESIGN DIMENSIONAL ARTS EMRAY, INC. McDONALD'S COPPER MOON KIESGEN

565

C ARRYING THE WEIGHT OF the world on their shoulders comes easy to Atlanta's sculpted strongmen.

Alle dinghe
Sijn mi te inghe:
Ic ben so wijdt.

Om een onghescepen
Hebbic ghegrepen
In eweghen tijt.

Ic hebt gheroen,
Het hoeft mi ontdaen
Widere dan witt:

Mi es te inghe al elc
Dat wette wel.
Ghi dies oec daer sijt.

All things
are too small
to hold me,
I am so vast

In the Infinite
I reach
for the Uncreated

I have
touched it,
it undoes me
wider than wide

Everything else
is too narrow

110

NAMED ONE OF THE TOP 10 works of 1980s American architecture by the American Institute of Architects, the High Museum captivates visitors with its impressive appearance as well as its array of exhibits. The museum is part of the Robert W. Woodruff Arts Center, which also includes the Atlanta Symphony Orchestra and the Atlanta College of Art.

ATLANTA'S COLORFUL ROADSIDE art is the cat's meow—even for man's best friend.

ATLANTA'S ARTISTIC VISIONARIES have garnered their share of international fame and accolades. Harry Callahan (TOP) changed the face of American photography, and, at the time of his death in 1999, was considered one of the greatest in his field. In addition to being a novelist, essayist, and columnist, Pearl Cleage (OPPOSITE) is also one of today's most popular African-American playwrights. And Radcliffe Bailey—long touted as one of Atlanta's best young artists—also seems bound for the path of stardom.

TALENT AND VISION ARE required to ensure a vital artistic future for Atlanta. The endeavors of area music students and artists such as Alicia Reymann (OPPOSITE) help contribute to the goal.

AMAZINGLY ENOUGH, THE visually spectacular Fox Theatre was almost demolished in the 1970s to make way for a skyscraper. Thanks to valiant preservation efforts on the part of Atlantans, the Fox is now the toast of the South, hosting a wide array of performances. On the docket every December is local favorite Atlanta Ballet's *The Nutcracker* (BOTTOM).

L ET'S FACE IT: WHAT'S HOT
and what's not have changed
drastically over the years, as
fashion diva and sometime Atlanta
resident Elton John (TOP) should
certainly know. Local designer
Wayne Van Nguyen (OPPOSITE)
keeps the fires lit under the city's
couture culture.

NOT ONES TO MASK THEIR individuality, Atlantans celebrate a diversity of talent. John McFall (OPPOSITE LEFT), artistic director for the Atlanta Ballet, also leads the Atlanta Ballet Centre for Dance Education. Honing a different sort of performance skill, puppeteer John Ludwig (OPPOSITE, BOTTOM RIGHT) serves as the associate artistic director for the Center for Puppetry Arts. Vintage clothier Rebecca Birdwhistell (OPPOSITE, TOP RIGHT)—owner of Stefan's Vintage Clothing in Little Five Points—travels the nation searching for special garments. And Shade Gallery owner John Gillett (ABOVE) showcases southern folk art.

ATLANTA

VERYTHING OLD IS NEW AGAIN, as modern technology mimics ancient remains displayed at the Fernbank Museum of Natural History.

WITH CROCODILE TEARS AND a lot of monkey business, Zoo Atlanta teaches kids of all ages to appreciate the variety of the wild kingdom. Founded in 1889, the zoo is home to many threatened and endangered animals, including red pandas, Sumatran tigers, and western lowland gorillas.

130

WHILE PIGS DON'T FLY IN Atlanta, they do enjoy a frosty mug of beer with a close friend every now and then. As for the rest of the city, well, it's just gone to the dogs, thanks in part to champion Frisbee catcher and professional model Sparky and his owner David Huffine (TOP).

ATLANT

THE CENTER FOR DISEASE Control in Atlanta (ABOVE LEFT) actively promotes the nation's good health through research that addresses diseases such as smallpox, Ebola virus, and AIDS. Also on a mission to save lives, prominent surgeon Dr. William Mitchell Jr. (OPPOSITE LEFT) provides invaluable skills and expertise to Piedmont Hospital.

A T L A N T A

THE ALMA MATER OF NOBEL laureate Dr. Martin Luther King Jr., Morehouse College confers bachelor's degrees on more African-American men each year than any other institution of higher learning in the nation. Under the leadership of President Walter E. Massey (OPPOSITE), the school ranks as the nation's only predominantly African-American all-male liberal arts college.

ATLANTA

TWO'S COMPANY WHEN ATLAN-
tans get together for festive
celebrations.

138

ATLANTA'S WORKFORCE RE-mains strong and competent, thanks in part to the number of roles held by groundbreaking women. Chief of Police Beverly Harvard (OPPOSITE LEFT) became the first African-American woman in the United States to run a major police department. CNN anchor Lynne Russell (OPPOSITE RIGHT) performs double duty as a licensed private investigator, sheriff's dep-uty, private bodyguard to visiting celebrities, and second-degree black belt in Choi Kwang Do. Leah Sears (ABOVE LEFT) gained promi-nence as the first African-American supreme court justice of the state of Georgia. And Margie Seals (ABOVE RIGHT), owner of the women-operated My Favorite Mechanic, makes her mark in a male-dominated field.

P UTTING HIS STRONG-ARM
tactics to good use, Altanta
native Evander Holyfield
(RIGHT) thrilled boxing fans by
becoming the world heavyweight
champion three consecutive times.
Former bodyguard Josh Patton
(OPPOSITE) has a pretty powerful
right hook himself. After losing
full swinging motion of his left
arm—the result of being slashed
with an ice pick while defending
his gangster boss in 1978—Patton
went on to become a two-time
champion in one-handed golf.

HELD EVERY SPRING, THE Georgia Renaissance Festival (OPPOSITE AND ABOVE LEFT) features musicians, minstrels, and magicians, as well as some action- packed jousting. Atlanta's world championship fencer Nhi Lan Le (ABOVE RIGHT) kept 1996 Olympic audiences on guard.

THE OCOEE RIVER (LEFT) IN Tennessee provided a tumultuous venue for Olympic white-water events, hosting enthusiasts from all over the world. But it was still waters that appealed to the late LeRoy Powell (OPPOSITE), a former cameraman who charmed Georgia with his unique television commentaries about the great outdoors.

T O ENJOY THE WEATHER, Atlantans head to the area's many beautiful parks. People blanket Piedmont Park (THIS PAGE), a perennial favorite during the annual Dogwood Festival, as well as on the rare snowy days of winter. Chastain Park (OPPOSITE) hosts many popular and classical concerts every summer in its outdoor amphitheater.

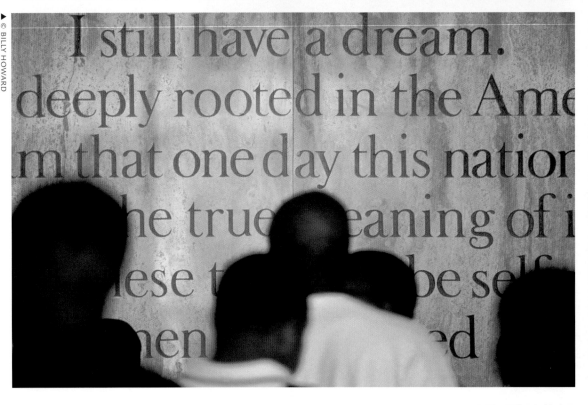

O N JANUARY 15, 1929, MARTIN Luther King Jr. was born at 501 Auburn Avenue (ABOVE) in the middle of the Sweet Auburn neighborhood. King would go on to play a pivotal role in the civil rights movement, touching the conscience of a generation. His charismatic personality has been remembered long after his death, and is epitomized in memorials such as Patrick Morelli's work *Behold* (OPPOSITE TOP), which is dedicated to King's memory. The statue depicts an African ritual in which a father lifts a newborn heavenward and proclaims, "Behold the only thing greater than yourself."

HEN DR. MARTIN LUTHER King Jr. was assassinated in Memphis on April 4, 1968, the world lost a courageous and selfless visionary. His legacy, however, lives on in Atlanta, from the Rev. Martin Luther King Jr. Center for Nonviolent Social Change to the annual celebrations of his life and works on a national holiday in his honor.

INSPIRED BY SUCH NOTED spiritual leaders as former Archbishop Desmond Tutu (OPPOSITE, TOP LEFT)—a Nobel laureate and recent visiting Emory University professor—Atlanta's families find comfort and strength in the scriptures.

PERPETUALLY REACHING toward the heavens, steeples reflecting the diversity of Atlanta's religious community dot the city's skyline.

ATLANTA

SOME 33,000 PEOPLE WORK at the William B. Hartsfield Atlanta International Airport, which—with its annual payroll of $1.7 billion—is considered the state's largest employer. The busiest passenger airport in the world, Hartsfield averages 2,000 departing and arriving flights a day.

Westbound   Eastbound ↓

PEACE SETTLES IN AT THE
end of a long business day,
and the hustle and bustle of
Atlanta's parking lots and MARTA
stations revert to a placid calm.

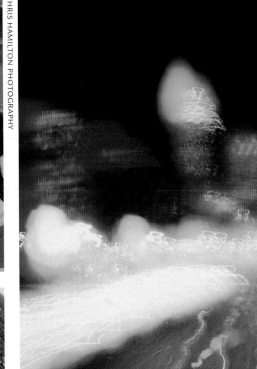

AT NIGHTFALL, THE ROADWAYS of Atlanta come alive with commuters on their way home to rest or with those just starting to get into the groove.

166

SNAKING ALONG THE HIGHWAYS and streets of the South, kudzu persistently defies any attempt at containment or destruction. Brought from Japan to prevent erosion, the mysteriously beautiful weed has taken over parts of the local landscape. Perhaps the enigmatic plant is a metaphor for Atlanta itself: With the right kind of courage, any trial or tribulation can be overcome.

ATLANTA

Profiles in Excellence

A look at the corporations, businesses, professional groups, and community service organizations that have made this book possible. Their stories—offering an informal chronicle of the local business community—are arranged according to the date they were established in the Atlanta area.

AGL RESOURCES INC.
AGNES SCOTT COLLEGE
AMC GLOBAL COMMUNICATIONS, INC.
ATLANTA TECHNICAL INSTITUTE
BASS HOTELS & RESORTS
BELLSOUTH CORPORATION
BUCKHEAD COALITION, INC.
THE CARTER CENTER
CATHEDRAL OF THE HOLY SPIRIT
THE COCA-COLA COMPANY
COCA-COLA ENTERPRISES INC.
CRAWFORD & COMPANY
DELTA AIR LINES
FEDERAL RESERVE BANK OF ATLANTA
GEORGIA-PACIFIC CORPORATION
THE HOME DEPOT®
INTERNET SECURITY SYSTEMS (ISS)
JACKSON SECURITIES INCORPORATED
KETCHUM ATLANTA
KING & SPALDING
THE LEADER PUBLISHING GROUP, INC.
MARIETTA CONFERENCE CENTER & RESORT
METROPOLITAN ATLANTA RAPID TRANSIT AUTHORITY (MARTA)
NATIONAL SERVICE INDUSTRIES, INC.
THE NORTH HIGHLAND COMPANY
PLATINUM TELEVISION GROUP
RARE HOSPITALITY INTERNATIONAL, INC.
ROLLINS, INC./ORKIN EXTERMINATING COMPANY, INC.
SCIENTIFIC-ATLANTA
SHERATON ATLANTA HOTEL
SHORTER COLLEGE
SIEMENS ENERGY & AUTOMATION, INC.
SOUTHERN COMPANY
SOUTHERN POLYTECHNIC STATE UNIVERSITY
TOWERY PUBLISHING, INC.
TURNER BROADCASTING SYSTEM, INC.
UNITED PARCEL SERVICE
WAFFLE HOUSE, INC.
WELLSTAR HEALTH SYSTEM
WESTIN PEACHTREE PLAZA HOTEL
THE WILLIAM B. HARTSFIELD ATLANTA INTERNATIONAL AIRPORT
WORLDSPAN®
YKK CORPORATION OF AMERICA

A T L A N T A

▼ © BUD LEE

THE RIGHT KIND OF COURAGE

AGL Resources Inc.

DRAMATIC EVENTS HAVE PUNCTUATED THE HISTORY OF AGL RESOURCES Inc. (AGLR), established by state charter as Atlanta Gas Light Company on February 16, 1856. The oldest business in Atlanta, this venerable company actually got its start two months earlier. On Christmas Day, 1855, Atlanta's first gas street lamp—one of 50—was lit to the cheers of hundreds of the young city's 6,000 residents, marking a significant sign of progress for the brash railroad town.

Although Atlanta Gas Light weathered the siege of Atlanta during the Civil War, its plant was eventually destroyed when Union troops set fire to the city in November 1864. Two years later, a rebuilt plant was up and running. Another dramatic change occurred on April 4, 1930, when the company switched from manufactured gas to natural gas, ushering in an era of cleaner, safer, and more economical fuel.

DEREGULATION COMES TO TOWN

Despite AGLR's colorful history, few events of the past can equal the impact of the Natural Gas Competition and Deregulation Act passed by the Georgia General Assembly in 1997. The deregulation of the industry allows competitors to enter the market and supply gas to the company's 1.45 million customers in more than 230 cities throughout Georgia. In addition, Atlanta Gas Light, AGLR's primary subsidiary, will continue to deliver, but not actually sell natural gas to customers. The

selling will be done by a number of gas marketers, giving consumers the chance to choose the products, price, and services that fit them best. "This is a monumental change that is transforming the company from a traditional utility to a competitive enterprise," says Walter M. Higgins, AGLR's chairman and chief executive officer. "Customers benefit from competition, and the new environment also offers opportunities to AGLR."

Anticipating deregulation, company leaders formed AGL Resources in 1994 as a holding company for a variety of energy-related businesses. Among them are Atlanta Gas Light Company, AGLR's natural gas utility; Georgia Natural Gas Services, which markets competitively priced natural gas products and services to residential, commercial, and industrial customers; a wholesale gas sales unit; a propane gas business; a consumer products division; and a retail energy sales business. Notes Higgins, "We are now a family of companies dedicated to profitable enterprise in an entirely new environment of competition in the energy industry."

GROWING FASTER

As deregulation spreads to other states, Georgia is serving as a model for the process—and AGLR is leading the way. In fact, the burgeoning trend toward deregulation promises to open up future markets for the Atlanta company and its subsidiaries. Higgins also expects growth through Georgia Natural Gas Services, which is positioned to capture a sizable share of the customers Atlanta Gas Light has served in the past. Further, AGLR plans to add new products through

both expansion and acquisition.

Looking to the future, Higgins anticipates a compound earnings growth of 6 to 7 percent from 1999 through 2004, considerably better than the figures regulated utilities have seen in recent years. How will AGLR achieve this level of success? According to Higgins, the company plans to follow three basic principles: "Don't chase last year's problems, but position the business to be a winner; make and keep a strong commitment to customers; and identify and measure the elements of success."

CLOCKWISE FROM TOP: ATLANTA GAS LIGHT COMPANY'S BLUE FLAME LOGO IS A FAMILIAR SIGHT THROUGHOUT GEORGIA.

WALTER M. HIGGINS SERVES AS CHAIRMAN AND CEO OF AGL RESOURCES INC.

ATLANTA GAS LIGHT COMPANY—AGL RESOURCES' LARGEST SUBSIDIARY, DELIVERING NATURAL GAS TO NEARLY 1.5 MILLION CUSTOMERS—IS GEORGIA'S OLDEST CORPORATE CITIZEN. TO HELP SYMBOLIZE THE COMPANY'S DEVOTION TO ITS HOME CITY, ATLANTA GAS LIGHT COMPANY AND WSB RADIO COSPONSOR THE SHINING LIGHT AWARD. JOINING FORMER GOVERNOR ZELL MILLER (SECOND FROM RIGHT) AT THE DEDICATION CEREMONY ARE (FROM LEFT) WALTER M. HIGGINS, CHAIRMAN AND CEO OF AGL RESOURCES; PAULA G. ROSPUT, PRESIDENT AND COO OF ATLANTA GAS LIGHT COMPANY; AND SCOTT SLADE, MORNING ANCHORMAN AT WSB RADIO.

WARREN BOND

ATLANTA

King & Spalding

FOR MORE THAN 110 YEARS, THE LAW FIRM OF KING & SPALDING (K&S) has provided high-caliber legal services to national and international clients. Established in Atlanta in 1885, the firm currently has more than 500 attorneys, 24 practice areas, and four offices in Atlanta, Houston, New York, and Washington, D.C. ❏ King & Spalding's client list is diverse, and includes more than 250 major U.S. companies,

among them nearly half of the Fortune 100 corporations. In addition, the firm represents mid-size companies and entrepreneurs, as well as government agencies and individuals from Europe, the Middle East, the Far East, and Latin America.

"Our clients are our best credentials," says Managing Partner Ralph B. Levy. "We take pride in the fact that K&S enjoys long-standing relationships with a great number of our clients." The firm has represented the Coca-Cola Company since the 1920s and has long-term relationships with SunTrust Banks, Inc. and Sprint Corporation. Its clients also include Delta Air Lines, General Motors, Home Depot, Lockheed Martin Corporation, Magellan Health Services, and Texaco.

ATTRACTING THE BEST AND THE BRIGHTEST

One of the outstanding characteristics of King & Spalding is the atmosphere of cooperation and camaraderie among the members. Notes Levy, "Our firm is based on collegial relationships among talented and professionally appealing people. We value strong partnering skills and loyalty to the institution, and we view these qualities as essential to our practice, profitability, and stability, and to providing professionally and personally enriching careers." Indeed, despite tremendous growth and the increasing pressures of competition, K&S has shown a stability rare in the legal profession today.

The firm makes a concerted effort to nurture its members. "We attract the best and the brightest," says Levy. "We want to keep them—and we do, not

only because of challenging work, but also because of our commitment to the continuous professional and personal development of all our attorneys." To accomplish this, the firm has established K&S University, its continuing legal education program; has its own in-house courtroom, which is used for training and trial preparation; and has developed the Link Program, a mentor program that provides guidance, assistance, and interaction among attorneys. This has proved effective in easing the transition of attorneys new to the firm.

Since its inception, King & Spalding has emphasized responsibility and commitment to the community. The firm supports a variety of local and national charitable, social, and civic endeavors. K&S was a key player in the effort to bring the 1996 Summer Olympic Games to Atlanta, and

the firm served as general counsel to the Atlanta Committee for the Olympic Games. K&S is also active in Habitat for Humanity in Atlanta and in the United Way.

King & Spalding's deep roots and enduring values are the keystones of the firm's long-term success. These same elements will ensure the firm's continuing excellence into the new millennium and beyond.

SINCE 1885, KING & SPALDING'S ATTORNEYS–INCLUDING (FROM LEFT) SAM NUNN, FORMER U.S. SENATOR AND PARTNER IN THE FIRM'S INTERNATIONAL PRACTICE; WALTER W. DRIVER JR., CHAIRMAN OF THE FIRM'S POLICY COMMITTEE AND PARTNER IN THE BANKING & FINANCE PRACTICE; CHILTON D. VARNER, MEMBER OF THE POLICY COMMITTEE AND PARTNER IN THE PRODUCT LIABILITY PRACTICE; AND RALPH B. LEVY, THE FIRM'S MANAGING PARTNER AND MEMBER OF THE POLICY COMMITTEE—HAVE PROVIDED HIGH-CALIBER LEGAL SERVICES TO NATIONAL AND INTERNATIONAL CLIENTS (TOP).

(FROM LEFT) FORMER U.S. ATTORNEY GENERAL JUDGE GRIFFIN BELL AND FORMER U.S. ATTORNEYS OF THE NORTHERN DISTRICT OF GEORGIA LARRY D. THOMPSON AND KENT B. ALEXANDER PRACTICE IN KING & SPALDING'S SPECIAL MATTERS/ GOVERNMENT INVESTIGATIONS PRACTICE GROUP (BOTTOM).

Southern Company

WITH NEARLY 50,000 MEGAWATTS OF ELECTRIC-GENERATING CAPACITY worldwide, Southern Company is the largest producer of electricity in the United States. In recent years, its reach has gone far beyond its southeastern roots to make it the fastest-growing electric utility in the country and one of the world's largest independent power producers. ❏ As the parent firm of Georgia Power, Alabama Power, Gulf Power,

Mississippi Power, and Savannah Electric, Southern Company supplies energy to more than 11 million people in most of Georgia and Alabama and parts of Mississippi and Florida. Its customers range from individuals in small homes to municipalities and vast manufacturing operations. Through its international affiliates, Southern Company-produced electricity is also lighting up homes and businesses in South America, Europe, and Asia.

Southern Company has annual operating revenues in the $12 billion range. To its shareholders' satisfaction, the company has paid an equal or increased dividend every quarter since its formation in 1948. It is frequently listed as one of the Fortune 500's most admired U.S. electric utilities.

Much of the company's recent growth has come from its pursuit of nontraditional businesses in the United States and from a push into overseas markets. Internationally, Southern Company focuses on Europe and Asia. "We look for those markets that provide real opportunities for growth. In Asia for example, the demand for electrical power is huge," says Chairman and CEO A.W. "Bill" Dahlberg. By 2002, at least 30 percent of Southern Company's earnings should be derived from these new business markets.

EFFECTIVE LEADERSHIP

Dahlberg is the man behind Southern Company's aggressive growth and new directions. He is known not only in Atlanta and the Southeast, but also throughout the industry for his visionary leadership, transforming a once-staid utility company into a dynamic worldwide player. Named CEO in 1995, Dahlberg has been with the company since 1960, when he took a job washing meter covers for Georgia Power.

With a down-to-earth style and good humor, Dahlberg is highly visible and very effective in supporting civic and social causes. He believes fervently that, as a corporate citizen, Southern Company has an obligation to the community. Dahlberg does the unexpected, whether leading the way to new business vistas for his company, or dressing up in a gorilla costume or silver space suit to grace the cover of Southern Company's annual report.

Under Dahlberg's leadership, Southern Company continues to grow despite changes in the industry. "As national and global energy markets continue to grow and expand, Southern Company expects to further strengthen its position and grow as a major player," says Dahlberg. "Although Atlanta will receive the same excellent, local service that we provided throughout the 20th century, the city will be energized

CEO BILL DAHLBERG HAS TRANSFORMED SOUTHERN COMPANY FROM A STAID UTILITY INTO AN ENERGETIC GROWTH COMPANY, WHILE SETTING AN EXAMPLE FOR HIS EMPLOYEES IN CORPORATE CITIZENSHIP.

by a multinational company in the 21st century."

POWERFUL ROOTS

Southern Company's roots are grounded in its five operating utilities, the largest of which is Georgia Power Company, based in Atlanta. Producing power from more than 60 plants—coal, nuclear, and hydro—Georgia Power generates and distributes power to almost 2 million customers in Georgia.

Georgia Power's beginnings go back to 1883 during Atlanta's days as an emerging city recovering from the Civil War. Led by banker Henry Atkinson, the City of Atlanta sold stock to raise $3,500 to purchase an electric light plant, which became the Georgia Electric Light Company of Atlanta. Several years later, the new generating plant was powering 800 streetlights and electric streetcars. In 1890, Atkinson gained control of the company, and for 40 years hereafter, in conjunction with

President Preston Arkwright, he led the company through rapid growth, expansion, and dramatic changes. In 1926, with the merging of several independent power companies— including the original Atlanta utility company that had evolved into Georgia Railway and Power Company—Georgia Power Company was formed.

A CITIZEN WHEREVER WE SERVE

In an address in 1927 to the National Electric Light Association in Atlantic City, Arkwright coined the phrase, A Citizen Wherever We Serve. To this day, it remains the core philosophy of Georgia Power. The company enjoys one of the highest customer satisfaction rates among all utilities in the country and is closely involved in many facets of the communities it serves, in business and economic development as well as civic and social efforts.

Georgia Power has long played a major role in the economic development of Atlanta and Georgia. The company's economic development professionals help local communities marshal and direct resources to attract new business. The group is active in a number of efforts, including government and public-private partnerships in developing policies to expand and improve Georgia's economic, educational, and environmental programs. "Bringing new business, jobs, and investments to Atlanta and Georgia is good for the company, the metro area, and the state," says David Ratcliffe, president of the company.

Through many years of service, Georgia Power has met challenges head-on. New opportunities lie ahead as competition increases, but the company is ready. The axiom Arkwright used more than 70 years ago is sure to ring true for the firm's next 100 years as well: A Citizen Wherever We Serve.

SOUTHERN COMPANY IS PLANTING 30 MILLION TREES ACROSS THE SOUTHEAST—THE LARGEST UTILITY-SPONSORED TREE-PLANTING PROGRAM IN THE NATION (LEFT).

SOUTHERN COMPANY, WHICH OPERATES NEARLY 50,000 MEGAWATTS OF GENERATION WORLDWIDE, IS A LEADER IN ENVIRONMENTAL RESEARCH. SINCE 1990, THE COMPANY HAS INVESTED MORE THAN $4 BILLION IN ENVIRONMENTAL CONTROL SYSTEMS, RESEARCH, AND DEVELOPMENT (RIGHT).

The Coca-Cola Company

THE BRIGHT, RED-AND-WHITE COCA-COLA LOGO IS ONE OF THE BEST-known trademarks in the world, recognized by an estimated 90 percent of the earth's population. The numbers are staggering: With some 6 billion people on earth, Coke is a product known by around 5.4 billion, and at least 1 billion consumers reach for a Coca-Cola product every day. From remote villages along the Amazon River and scientific stations in Antarctica to delicatessens in New York, noodle shops in Tokyo, and cafés along the Champs Élysées, the slogans ring true: Coke Is It. It's the Real Thing. Things Go Better with Coke. It's Always Coca-Cola.

In 1891, Asa G. Candler acquired complete ownership of the Coca-Cola business and registered the trademark in 1893. Two years later, at the annual meeting, Candler stood before stockholders to announce that "Coca-Cola is now drunk in every state and territory in the United States" (TOP).

From its headquarters in Atlanta, the Coca-Cola Company maintains a global presence through its widely recognized, red-and-white logo (BOTTOM).

PRODUCTS PEOPLE KNOW

The ubiquitous cola drink in various forms—Coca-Cola, Diet Coke, and Cherry Coke, along with their caffeine-free versions—is the company's flagship product, composing approximately 68 percent of its worldwide beverage shipments. In the United States and, of course, in Atlanta, Coca-Cola classic is the number-one-selling soft drink.

While Coca-Cola is the world's leading soft drink, the company produces many other familiar beverages. For example, Diet Coke is the world's leading no-calorie product. Introduced in 1961, Sprite, the world's leading lemon-lime soft drink, is the fourth-best-selling soft drink of any kind. Developed in Europe during World War II, Fanta is the world's leading orange-flavored soft drink and the second-best-selling soft drink outside the United States. The Coca-Cola Company markets more than 190 products worldwide, including POWERaDE, Nestea, Fruitopia, Citra, Surge, Barq's, Minute Maid soft drinks, Fresca, and Mr. Pibb.

The Coca-Cola Company also owns the Minute Maid Company, the world's largest marketer of juice and juice-drink products. Minute Maid orange juice, lemonade, and other fruit drinks are all familiar to consumers. For kids, Hi-C is a favorite beverage.

As people consume various Coca-Cola products, stockholders rejoice. Since the company first sold stock publicly in 1919, Coca-Cola shares have accumulated exponential value despite cyclical changes in the U.S. and global economies. Out of modest investors, millionaires have been made, and Coke is one of the most coveted stocks on the market.

FROM A KETTLE IN THE BACKYARD

From a little drugstore in downtown Atlanta to a global powerhouse, Coca-Cola's history is the stuff of legend. Coke was formulated by pharmacist John Stith Pemberton, who, in May 1886, first mixed the caramel-colored concoction in a brass kettle in the backyard of his home on Marietta Street. Distribution as he knew it was carrying a gallon jug of syrup down the street to Jacob's Pharmacy. By design or by accident, Pemberton's syrup was mixed with carbonated water and the famous fizzy drink was born.

His partner and bookkeeper, Frank M. Robinson, suggested the name Coca-Cola and penned the distinctive flowing script. That first year, the drugstore sold an average of nine Coca-Cola drinks each day, and Pemberton sold 25 gallons of syrup, shipped in bright red wooden kegs. Red has been the Coke color ever since.

The refreshing drink would have remained a mere local favorite without the marketing wizardry of Atlanta entrepreneur Asa G. Candler. By 1891, he had acquired complete ownership of the Coca-Cola business. In 1893, he registered the trademark, and two years later, at the annual meeting, Candler stood before stockholders to announce that "Coca-Cola is now drunk in every state and territory in the United States."

Widespread distribution was made possible by the bottling innovation of candy merchant

Joseph A. Biederharn of Mississippi, who wanted to take the fountain drink to a picnic. Large-scale bottling began in 1899, and the original system of using local bottling and canning operations continues today as the company sells its syrups and concentrates to bottling businesses around the world.

The turn of the century marked the beginning of the company's global presence. Compliments of Candler's son Charles, Coca-Cola made its way to London when he ventured there on vacation. The distinctive green-glass bottle was designed in 1915 to make Coke stand out among its competitors.

In 1919, a group of Atlanta investors, led by banker Ernest Woodruff, bought the Coca-Cola Company for $25 million. His son, Robert W. Woodruff, soon became head of the company. Over the next five decades, the outspoken, cigar-smoking magnate led the company to new heights and new products, and to innovations in packaging and distributing, in-

cluding the six-bottle carton and the automatic fountain dispenser.

AGGRESSIVE, WORLDWIDE EXPANSION

Through the 1980s and early 1990s, the company grew under the leadership of the late Roberto Goizueta, who dramatically expanded its global reach, its products, and its value. The company's market share increased to more than 45 percent of the $55 billion U.S. soft drink market and more than 51 percent of the worldwide soft drink market. Currently, more than 60 percent of the company's volume and 70 percent of its profits are outside the United States. The Coca-Cola Company has become a textbook study in mastering the challenges in marketing and advertising to a diverse world population.

In 1999, the company made a bold move acquiring parts of London-based Cadbury Schweppes' international beverage business. This giant step extended the Coca-Cola Company's reach even

further and added a cornucopia of brands, including top sellers Schweppes, Canada Dry, Dr Pepper, and Crush. The nearly $1 billion deal covers more than 160 countries. Heading the worldwide expansion is Chairman and CEO M. Douglas Ivester.

Atlanta has benefited tremendously from the support of its hometown company. Social and civic causes and organizations, education, the arts, and sports all know the generosity of the Coca-Cola Company. The company has been a sponsor of the Olympics since 1928, huge events such as the Tour de France and World Cup Soccer, and community-based events and causes. From down the street in Atlanta to across the globe, consumers agree that It's Always Coca-Cola.

IN 1999, THE COCA-COLA COMPANY EXTENDED ITS GLOBAL REACH BY ACQUIRING PARTS OF LONDON-BASED CADBURY SCHWEPPES' BEVERAGE BUSINESS. HEADED BY CHAIRMAN AND CEO M. DOUGLAS IVESTER, THIS GIANT STEP ADDED A CORNUCOPIA OF WIDELY RECOGNIZED BRANDS TO THE COMPANY'S ROSTER, INCLUDING TOP SELLERS SCHWEPPES, CANADA DRY, DR PEPPER, AND CRUSH (TOP LEFT).

FROM CHINA (TOP LEFT) TO BANGLADESH (TOP RIGHT) TO NEPAL (BOTTOM LEFT) TO ARGENTINA (BOTTOM RIGHT), COKE IS A PRODUCT KNOWN BY AROUND 5.4 BILLION CONSUMERS, AND AT LEAST 1 BILLION REACH FOR A COCA-COLA PRODUCT EVERY DAY.

Agnes Scott College

INCE ITS FOUNDING IN 1889, AGNES SCOTT COLLEGE HAS BEEN CULTIVATING leaders such as Rhodes and Fulbright scholars, state supreme court justices, physicians, educators, scientists, artists, and corporate leaders. ❏ A commitment to superior women's education and an unusually challenging academic environment make the college's name synonymous with quality. Recently, *Kaplan/Newsweek's College Catalog*

rankedAgnes Scott as one of the top women's colleges in the nation in its 2000 Schools for the Academically Competitive Student ranking.

LEARN FROM THE BEST

At Agnes Scott College, 100 percent of the regular full-time faculty hold the highest degree in their fields; the school's professors are experts and scholars. Among this distinguished group are Harvard, Stanford, University of California-Berkeley, Yale, and Duke graduates. They stay current in their disciplines by researching, networking with colleagues, and publishing in numerous academic journals.

Students work with professors on original research projects, gaining firsthand experience in their majors and presenting their findings at conferences. At Agnes Scott, a student-faculty ratio of 10-to-1 means that each student gets individual attention and each professor can act as a mentor.

Agnes Scott students can develop a better understanding of themselves through study abroad, which is an integral part of the Agnes Scott experience. The opportunities for study abroad, the presence of international students and scholars on campus, and collaborations with partner organizations around the world contribute to the education of globally competent citizens. The college sponsors two types of faculty-led study tours: the Global Awareness program, which focuses on non-European countries like Mexico, Japan, Ghana, and China; and the Global Connections program in Nicaragua, India, Greece, Ireland, and France. In addition, the college sponsors exchange and affiliate programs at more than 130 institutions located in 40 countries.

Students can fulfill academic requirements choosing from 28 majors, 27 minors, dual-degree programs, concentrations in business and education, and a dozen special curricular programs. The college also offers a master of arts in teaching secondary English.

As far as technology is concerned, Agnes Scott has made sure it remains at the forefront. A computer network with an automated library and interactive learning center, a multimedia classroom, a Macintosh lab, and Internet access are provided to enhance student performance.

To meet the changing needs of higher education, a $100 million expansion and renovation of the campus is under way.

EXTRACURRICULAR ACTIVITIES

Most Agnes Scott students balance their studies with participation in campus and volunteer organizations. The college makes it easy for them to try new activities and pursue long-standing interests by sponsoring dozens of extracurricular groups.

Among these activities are sports teams; volunteer opportunities; Honor Court and Student

Government Association; the *Profile*, a student-run campus newspaper; the Blackfriars theater group; and many more. For every possible interest or organization, there is a student leadership role to be filled.

IN METROPOLITAN ATLANTA

Though the beautiful Agnes Scott campus is located on approximately 100 acres in a national historic district and residential neighborhood in Decatur, Georgia, the college is integrally linked to Atlanta. Downtown Atlanta lies just six miles from campus, so it's easy to reach the cultural, sports, business, and social centers within the city.

Agnes Scott's location in Atlanta allows students to try on several career hats, gaining experience and contacts in their disciplines. The college's career planning office provides more than 250 internship opportunities in finance, sciences, arts, journalism, and many other fields.

The Atlanta Semester, a program unique to Agnes Scott College, focuses on women, leadership, and social change in the city, and invites students worldwide to join the campus community for a semester. In addition to specialized courses, students attend speakers' forums, network with Atlanta leaders, and intern in the business and non-profit communities.

SPRINGBOARD FOR SUCCESS

Agnes Scott President Mary Brown Bullock is one of the college's many successful alumnae. These women share a drive to succeed, a limitless curiosity, and a propensity for leadership.

The college considers its graduates the truest measure of an Agnes Scott education. It boasts Georgia's first female Rhodes Scholar, five consecutive Fulbright scholars, two Goldwater scholars, television newscasters, a NASA engineer, a Pulitzer Prize-winning author, a Tony Award-winning playwright, a former governor of the Federal Reserve Board, CEOs, writers, educators, and community activists.

The Agnes Scott student body is comprised of a diverse group of approximately 900 women from all over the United States and 29 countries around the world. They are academically successful, active in extracurricular activities, and passionate about succeeding in college, community, and life.

Once at Agnes Scott, students discover course work that stretches their minds, opinions, and beliefs. They make friends who inspire and motivate them, developing a social life to balance academics. Ultimately, students optimize all the opportunities to make a difference in the community and to establish footholds for a fulfilling career after graduation.

▲ STEWART COHEN

▲ STEWART COHEN

▲ GARY MEEK

CLOCKWISE FROM TOP LEFT:
AGNES SCOTT STUDENTS MAKE FRIENDS WHO INSPIRE AND MOTIVATE THEM, DEVELOPING A SOCIAL LIFE TO BALANCE ACADEMICS.

STUDENTS CAN FULFILL ACADEMIC REQUIREMENTS CHOOSING FROM 28 MAJORS AND 27 MINORS.

STUDENTS WORK ON ORIGINAL RESEARCH PROJECTS, GAINING FIRST-HAND EXPERIENCE IN THEIR MAJORS AND OFTEN PRESENTING THEIR FINDINGS AT CONFERENCES.

THE COLLEGE'S MANY SUCCESSFUL GRADUATES SHARE A DRIVE TO SUCCEED AND A PROPENSITY FOR LEADERSHIP.

THE BEAUTIFUL CAMPUS IS LOCATED ON APPROXIMATELY 100 ACRES IN A NATIONAL HISTORIC DISTRICT.

Federal Reserve Bank of Atlanta

THE FEDERAL RESERVE BANK OF ATLANTA HAS BEEN A MAJOR FEATURE in Atlanta's business and financial landscape for more than 85 years. The Atlanta Fed is part of the U.S. Federal Reserve System, the central bank of the United States, which establishes monetary policy, supervises and regulates banks, and operates a nationwide payments system. ❏ With 11 sister banks in the Federal Reserve System, the

THE FEDERAL RESERVE BANK OF ATLANTA HAS BEEN A MAJOR FEATURE IN ATLANTA'S BUSINESS AND FINANCIAL LANDSCAPE FOR MORE THAN 85 YEARS. THE ATLANTA FED IS PART OF THE FEDERAL RESERVE SYSTEM, THE CENTRAL BANK OF THE UNITED STATES, WHICH ESTABLISHES MONETARY POLICY, SUPERVISES AND REGULATES BANKS, AND OPERATES A NATIONWIDE PAYMENTS SYSTEM.

Atlanta Fed serves the Sixth Federal Reserve District, which encompasses Alabama, Florida, Georgia, and portions of Louisiana, Mississippi, and Tennessee. In the 1990s, the Atlanta institution also took on supervisory responsibility for U.S. operations of banks headquartered in Latin America and the Caribbean. This job includes monitoring the U.S. offices of these banks and the economies and regulatory systems in their home countries. More recently, the Atlanta Fed assumed the lead role in a nationwide effort to make checks and other methods of retail payment more efficient through greater use of electronics.

On a regular basis, the Federal Reserve Bank of Atlanta president meets with the presidents of other regional Federal Reserve banks, as well as the seven governors of the board in Washington, D.C., to discuss and decide monetary issues and the direction of interest rates. To support its input, the Atlanta Fed draws on the expertise of its more than 15 staff economists, who conduct ongoing research and analysis of current issues in the Southeast and the nation. The bank also draws on the insights its 44 directors— business and community leaders from around the District—bring to bear on current economic conditions.

THE FEDERAL RESERVE SYSTEM

The establishment of the Federal Reserve System, under Woodrow Wilson's presidency, was a hard-won political battle. The measure for a central banking system passed on December 23, 1913, and was followed by intense competition among cities throughout the country to be one of the 12 Federal Reserve Bank loca-

tions. In 1914, Atlanta's Chamber of Commerce, bankers, and business leaders joined forces to present their case to the Federal Reserve's organization committee, which was charged with selecting the sites. Atlanta then, as now, was able to tout its status as a transportation hub, its role as a business and financial center, and the growing number of manufacturers and distributors locating in the area.

"THE BIGGEST THING"

Then the heart of the South's all-important cotton industry, Atlanta won its bid to the organization committee. It was a critical success for the Deep South, and one banker of the day summed up the feelings of the rejoicing city: "This bank will enable us of the Southeast to finance our own needs. . . . It is the biggest thing for this section that has happened in a long time."

The presence of the Federal Reserve Bank of Atlanta continues to be significant, as it processes a huge and growing volume of payments—cash, check, and electronic—supervises many southeastern banks, and monitors the pulse of the economy. The bank makes its extensive research available to the public through publications, speeches, conferences on policy issues, and participation in public policy organizations.

After more than 80 years on the same site in downtown Atlanta, the Federal Reserve Bank of Atlanta is moving to a new complex in Midtown in order to meet its needs for more space. The familiar great bronze eagle, perched atop its marble column from the bank's original 1918 structure, will watch over Atlanta's businesses and industries at the new location, scheduled to open in 2001.

O MARK THE 70TH ANNIVERSARY OF PASSENGER SERVICE ON JUNE 17, 1999, Delta Air Lines re-created its very first flight, using a restored single-engine, five-passenger Travel Air plane. Dramatic progress in air transportation has unfolded since that auspicious beginning. Today, the once five-hour flight from Dallas to Jackson, Mississippi takes an hour and a half. Sleek, silver jets now soar at speeds of 574 miles per hour, cruise above the clouds at more than 30,000 feet, and rely on sophisticated instruments for navigation instead of a visual spotting of local landmarks like lakes, fields, and water towers.

In 1999, 106 million customers flew Delta, more than any other airline in the world. Currently, more than 100 million people annually board Delta's hundreds of planes bound for destinations in its global network of 350 cities in nearly 60 countries. And Delta's Atlanta Worldport is the largest single-carrier hub in the world. The airline's U.S. network also includes four other geographically strategic hubs in Cincinnati, Dallas-Fort Worth, Salt Lake City, and New York-Kennedy.

BOLL WEEVIL BEGINNINGS

I n 1924, Delta began as a crop dusting service, Huff Daland Dusters, in Macon to battle the destructive boll weevil that was ravaging the South's vital cotton crop. Within a few years, the little company owned 18 planes and had the largest private fleet in the world. It soon added mail service and passenger service to balance its seasonal crop dusting business, and in 1929, with the launching of passenger service, changed its name to Delta Air Service, after the Mississippi Delta region it served.

In 1941, Delta relocated its headquarters to Atlanta, a choice based on the city's central location in the South and on a growing number of routes that included Atlanta as both a destination and a transfer point. That year, the airline employed 400 people, had five small passenger planes, flew to 16 cities—primarily in the Southeast—and served more than 58,000 customers.

WORLDWIDE DESTINATIONS

D elta's growth has soared through expansions of routes, as well as acquisitions and mergers with other carriers, including Northeast Airlines in 1972, Western Airlines in 1987, and Pan American World Airway's North Atlantic routes in 1991. Additionally, in 1955, Delta pioneered the hub-and-spoke system, which many airlines in the industry use today.

COURTESY OF THE DELTA AIR TRANSPORT HERITAGE MUSEUM

The carrier inaugurated its first transatlantic service in April 1978 with a flight from Atlanta to London. In recent years, Delta has pursued international routes aggressively, including rapid development into Latin America. The carrier's Atlanta hub is a natural "to capture a significant amount of the fast-growing traffic to Central and South America," says a company report. Through additions of new routes and through code sharing and strategic alliances with leading international airlines, such as Air France in Europe, AeroPeru and AeroMexico in Latin America, and China Southern Airlines in China, the airline's global reach continues to expand.

According to Delta President and Chief Executive Officer Leo F. Mullin, alliances between airlines are critical in competing in an increasingly global industry as a way to "get customers from anywhere to everywhere. Airline alliances are revolutionizing the nature of worldwide competition, and Delta intends to be a leader as these changes occur."

IN 1929, HUFF DALAND DUSTERS CHANGED ITS NAME TO DELTA AIR SERVICE—AFTER THE MISSISSIPPI DELTA REGION IT SERVED—WITH THE LAUNCHING OF PASSENGER SERVICE. NOW OPERATING AS DELTA AIR LINES, THE COMPANY RESTORED ONE OF ITS EARLIEST PASSENGER AIRPLANES, A FIVE-PASSENGER TRAVEL AIR, AND, RECENTLY, A 21-PASSENGER DC-3.

IN THE 1940S, DELTA AIR LINES LOCATED ITS GENERAL OFFICE IN ATLANTA. AT THAT TIME, THE AIRLINE EMPLOYED 400 PEOPLE; HAD FIVE SMALL PASSENGER PLANES, INCLUDING THE DELTA DC-3; AND FLEW TO 16 CITIES, PRIMARILY IN THE SOUTHEAST.

National Service Industries, Inc.

A LARGER-THAN-LIFE BRONZE SCULPTURE DOMINATES THE GRANITE AND glass rotunda of the Midtown Atlanta headquarters of National Service Industries, Inc. (NSI). A compelling piece of art, *Winning* captures a runner in three poses at critical seconds of his race: crouched and ready in the starting position; racing forward at full stride; and finally, arms upstretched, exalting in victory.

Created by sculptor Richard McDermott Miller, *Winning* evokes the spirit of NSI.

Below the sculpture is a plaque that bears these words: "At National Service Industries, winning is one of our strongest motivating forces. Winning means setting difficult goals and meeting them. It means concentrating our efforts on the business we know best to produce superior returns to our shareholders. It means having a corporate culture that fosters innovation, embraces change, and encourages employees to reach their full potential. As the company builds strength upon strength, we remain dedicated to serving the needs of our customers and maintaining the highest standards of excellence."

A JOURNEY TO HIGH PERFORMANCE

Founded in 1919 as Atlanta Linen Company, NSI currently has four business segments: lighting equipment, textile rental, chemicals, and envelopes. Several companies represent NSI in these fields. Lithonia Lighting Company is a manufacturer of lighting fixtures and equipment for architectural, commercial, industrial, and residential customers. National Linen Service is one of the largest textile rental suppliers in the United States. NSI has several companies that manufacture and market cleaning, water treatment, and insecticide products: Zep Manufacturing Company, Enforcer Products, Inc., Selig Chemical

Industries, and National Chemical. NSI's Atlantic Envelope Company is the third-largest U.S. producer of custom envelopes and specialty filing products.

Throughout its long history, National Service Industries has, at various times, acquired and divested businesses. Since 1996, however, the company has focused on these four core services as it pursues its goal to move from being a solid performer to being a high performer. Says Chairman, President, and CEO James S. Balloun, "That means we want to reach the high-performance range of the Standard & Poor's 500. To do so, NSI needs to deliver total returns of 14 percent annually, over time." Over the last several

A COMPELLING PIECE OF ART, *WINNING* CAPTURES A RUNNER IN THREE POSES AT CRITICAL SECONDS OF HIS RACE: CROUCHED AND READY IN THE STARTING POSITION; RACING FORWARD AT FULL STRIDE; AND FINALLY, ARMS UPSTRETCHED, EXALTING IN VICTORY CREATED BY SCULPTOR RICHARD MCDERMOTT MILLER, *WINNING* EVOKES THE SPIRIT OF NATIONAL SERVICE INDUSTRIES, INC. (NSI).

years, returns have been in the 11 to 13 percent range. Annual sales for the publicly held company are more than $2 billion. With the 1999 acquisition of Holophane Corporation, revenues are expected to approach $2.5 billion.

A Watershed Year

Nineteen ninety-six was a watershed year for National Service Industries. Balloun joined NSI as the top executive, following several years of changing leadership at the company. Prior to that time, NSI had excelled under the stable and popular leadership of Erwin Zaban for 26 years. But in the early 1990s, for the first time since its founding, the company suffered a decline in performance after years of steady growth.

Taking the helm with decisiveness and vision, Balloun began the journey to high performance and set the goal to become a company of choice. To progress along that path meant changing virtually every aspect of the company, including the basic corporate culture. According to Balloun, the very high performers manage to become companies of choice for three critical groups of people: employees, customers, and shareholders.

A Virtue of Plain-Vanilla Businesses

With the assistance of a strong leadership team, Balloun is guiding the company along its journey. "We see our job as making a virtue of plain-vanilla businesses—getting more performance out of them than competitors do," he says. Management has set high goals for the company that will be measured in economic profit, and long-term incentives are aligned with those goals. NSI is investing energy and effort in leadership at all levels of the company, and it is promoting the values of a high-performance organization, including more extensive teamwork, employee recognition, communication, an emphasis on personal performance and growth, and a sense of ownership.

Founded in Atlanta in 1919, National Service Industries, Inc. (NSI) has a growing national presence and is directing efforts toward the international scene as well.

Says Balloun, "We took a hard look at NSI's holdings, and we divested some of our rental operations. The four business segments we have are those which we believe we can grow profitably." The company is among the top three competitors in each of its markets, but none of the businesses has more than a 13 percent share. "That means opportunity. That means room to grow. We're also looking beyond these four businesses for other strong growth platforms," says Balloun.

NSI has a growing national presence through internal development, as well as through acquisition within the four segments. And the firm is directing efforts toward the international scene as well, albeit cautiously. "Because we have a lot of opportunity in North America, we are taking a somewhat cautious approach to international expansion," comments Balloun. He adds that NSI's strongest international efforts are in Europe and Central and South America, and the company is exploring additional possibilities in Asia.

Words of Passage

There are three words that describe the passage NSI is going through to achieve its vision: imagine, reach, and become. These words have become part of the company's lexicon and have appeared as themes in its annual reports. The word for the 1999 report, which follows NSI's acquisition of Holophane—the largest acquisition in years—is advance.

"We used 'imagine' when we were developing the vision for NSI, 'reach' as we stretched to accomplish higher goals, and 'become' as we built high-performance values across our companies and changed the fundamental nature of our organization. Now we're emphasizing 'advance' as our current challenge," says Balloun. "It is an exciting journey."

The William B. Hartsfield Atlanta International Airport

THE WILLIAM B. HARTSFIELD ATLANTA INTERNATIONAL AIRPORT IS THE busiest passenger airport in the world. It serves a staggering number of people coming from and going to destinations all over the United States and the world. More than 213,000 passengers go through Atlanta's airport daily, totaling 78.1 million people each year. More than 2,493 cargo and passenger flights take off and land on the airport's busy runways every day, totaling about 909,911 flights annually.

In 1925, several visionary business leaders in Atlanta, led by a young city alderman, William Berry Hartsfield (1890-1971), committed the city to lease an abandoned auto racetrack and turn it into an airfield, thus setting the stage for Atlanta's long-standing prominence as an air transportation hub. The 287-acre field was named Candler Field after its former owner, Coca-Cola magnate Asa Candler. A year later, the first flight, delivering mail from Florida, landed in Atlanta. In 1930, Delta Air Service, now Delta Air Lines, flew its first passengers into Candler Field. The carrier, which is today the largest single airline at the airport, moved its headquarters from Monroe, Louisiana, to Atlanta in 1941.

Hartsfield went on to become mayor of Atlanta for nearly 24 years, and he holds a place in the city's history as one of its most notable and long-serving mayors. Throughout his tenure, he promoted Atlanta as an air hub. With his backing, the renamed (in 1946) Atlanta Municipal Airport touted a list of firsts: first airport to have an air passenger terminal, an air control tower, and an instrument landing system. Fittingly, when Atlanta's present, 2.5 million-square-foot terminal opened in 1980, it was named for the man considered the father of aviation in Atlanta.

Since the first international flight by the now defunct Eastern Airlines to Montreal in 1956, and the arrival of Sabena Belgian World Airlines as Hartsfield's first international carrier in 1978, more and more of the world is at Atlanta's doorstep. Flights in and out of Atlanta carry people and goods to and from more than 32 countries in North and South America, Europe, and Asia, as well as Australia.

MONICA NIKORE

THE WILLIAM B. HARTSFIELD ATLANTA INTERNATIONAL AIRPORT IS THE BUSIEST PASSENGER AIRPORT IN THE WORLD. IT SERVES A STAGGERING NUMBER OF PEOPLE COMING FROM AND GOING TO DESTINATIONS ALL OVER THE UNITED STATES AND THE WORLD.

MONICA NIKORE

CITY WITHIN A CITY

Metro Atlanta and its airport enjoy a symbiotic relationship. Certainly, access via air to so many areas of the country and the world has contributed significantly to Atlanta's strong growth and robust economy. In turn, the bustling business of Atlanta has fueled the airport's growth in both passenger and cargo service. "Atlanta's increasing visibility as a world-class city and Hartsfield as the airport that brings the world within reach

have a profound effect on metro Atlanta and the entire region," says Ben DeCosta, general manager of the airport.

The airport's role is critical to the continued expansion of business in Atlanta. Says DeCosta, "Our job is to make sure that Hartsfield Atlanta International Airport expands safely, efficiently, and profitably to meet the demands of its customers. This helps us to achieve our mission of being the best airport by exceeding customers' expectations." He is currently spearheading the implementation of a 20-year master plan that will ensure that the airport meets those demands into 2015.

Hartsfield—just 10 miles south of downtown and spread over 3,750 acres—is a city within a city, owned and operated by the City of Atlanta. This municipality's main economy is the movement of people and goods by air. It must serve not only those people who pass through its gates, but also its tenants, the airlines that are the core of its existence. The same extent of businesses and services used to manage a small city are required to effectively operate the airport. Utilities, security, public transportation, food services, shopping, and parking are among the numerous services needed to successfully maintain its operations. Add to these the unique need to provide every measure possible for safety in the busy skies above.

Hartsfield Atlanta International

Airport is the largest employment center in Georgia, with approximately 43,300 direct airport-generated jobs, including airline, ground transportation, concession-aire, security, federal government, City of Atlanta, and airport tenant employees. The economic impact of Hartsfield extends throughout the region, and some 471,500 jobs in the area are directly related to airport services. Translated into dollars, the total annual regional economic impact of the airport is close to $15 billion.

LOOKING TO THE FUTURE

It's no wonder that, given Hartsfield's great impact on and importance to the region in so many ways, Atlanta is looking to the future and how the airport can continue to serve an ever increasing flow of air travelers and cargo. While the current number of passengers annually is about

78 million, projections indicate that by 2015, some 121 million passengers will come through the airport.

The Hartsfield Airport Master Plan calls for a transformation of the facility, with new terminals, concourses, cargo facilities, and roadways. There are plans for a new runway to add to its existing four; the fifth runway is expected to open in 2005. "Over the next 10 years, our capital program involves the spending of $5.4 billion on various additions, changes, and improvements to the airport," notes DeCosta. "These are all critical things we are undertaking to make sure we meet the demands of our customers and tenants. Substantial growth of passengers and cargo is a given. We have a vision for what this airport must be to keep up with and exceed future needs and demands."

MORE THAN 200,000 PASSENGERS GO THROUGH ATLANTA'S AIRPORT DAILY, TOTALING 78.1 MILLION PEOPLE EACH YEAR (TOP LEFT AND RIGHT).

MORE THAN 2,493 CARGO AND PASSENGER FLIGHTS TAKE OFF AND LAND ON THE AIRPORT'S BUSY RUNWAYS EVERY DAY, TOTALING ABOUT 909,911 FLIGHTS ANNUALLY (BOTTOM).

Crawford & Company

AROUND THE WORLD, WHEN NATURAL DISASTERS STRIKE AND LEAVE devastation in their wake, Crawford & Company is ready for action. After a hurricane, tornado, flood, or earthquake, Crawford's loss adjusters are among the first people into disaster areas to help rebuild shattered lives. Their job is to assess property damage and initiate the process for the insured to obtain funds for repair and

rebuilding. Although perhaps the most visible and dramatic of its services, catastrophe services are just one of the many offerings from this Atlanta-based risk and claims management company.

LOCAL BUSINESS ON A GLOBAL SCALE

The company traces its modest beginnings to May 1941, when young, ambitious James H. Crawford set up his two-man office in Columbus, Georgia, with a secondhand desk and typewriter. In 1946, Crawford established an office in Atlanta, and since then, his company has grown into a

vast, global network, becoming the world's largest independent risk and claims management organization in a highly competitive industry. With 700-plus offices in the United States and more than 65 other countries, the company employs more than 10,000 professionals. In addition to general loss-adjusting, Crawford provides claims management services for workers' compensation, disability, and long-term care; liability, including auto and product liability, and class action settlements; property claims management services for personal and commercial property; catastrophe services for man-made environmental losses and natural disasters; managed care services; and information management and analysis.

"This is a people business every step of the way, and we interact with a real cross section of men and women in all walks of life and in many different cultures," says Archie Meyers Jr., who began with the company as a casualty adjuster in 1959.

"Crawford has been in risk and claims management a long time," adds Meyers. "We have learned and adapted along the way, and as a result, we are very good at the basics of this business." Indeed, those basics were set out by founder Jim Crawford himself in late 1948 in his General Memorandum No. 1. It was a mission statement before that term entered the business lexicon, and the document is often cited to this day. Wrote Crawford, "To turn out a top-quality job—always. To report promptly, accurately and concisely. To remember we are a service organization and are always available when needed. To be courteous, polite and business-

like at all times. To be under obligation to and accept favors from no man."

"That philosophy is the foundation of our business," says Meyers. He also cites the company's fundamental strengths— local expertise, the ability to customize services, and technological agility—as the underpinnings of Crawford's current success and future expansion.

The company's increasingly wide global presence is broken into four key regions: the United States; the Americas, including Canada, Mexico, and the Caribbean; the United Kingdom, Europe, and Africa; and the Asia Pacific region. But Crawford prides itself on its local expertise. "We have a broader geographic spread than any other independent risk and claims management service provider, with a service infrastructure that supports local expertise at every level," notes Meyers. Crawford professionals at the local level understand the character, legalities, and jurisdictional requirements of their particular markets, from the Big Apple and

London to small towns in Iowa or Germany.

EQUIPPED TO RESPOND

Like a film director calling for a scene to begin, Crawford people spring into action when customers experience a catastrophic loss or widespread exposure. Literally at a moment's notice, the company must be prepared to set up a full-service, on-site operation, at times in multiple locations. "This is our forte," comments Meyers. "Crawford can orchestrate a response strategy that enables us to process thousands of claims and quickly resolve situations."

These events can be massive, like Hurricane Georges, a major earthquake, or a huge oil spill; or smaller, such as a local ice storm, wildfire, or property fire. The reason Crawford can move so quickly, explains Meyers, is that the company utilizes its people, processes, technology, experience, and infrastructure to tailor its approach to meet the customer's specific problem or operation.

Traditionally a low-tech, people-intensive business, claims process-

ing has entered a new dimension with continually—and rapidly—advancing technology. "Data is all-important for the next generation of claims processing," says Meyers. Crawford has focused on a data storehouse in a central location, allowing the company to produce customized reports and analysis on demand.

"Our future lies in keeping up with and utilizing technology to its fullest," comments Meyers. In addition, there are many opportunities for further growth. The company expects to expand in the

international arena, managed care industry, public entity market, and catastrophe market, and through worldwide outsourcing opportunities and class action services.

"Since Jim Crawford founded this business, Crawford & Company has set the standards for the industry. In fact, we are considered the trainers for the industry," says Meyers. "We expect to continue to fly the standard of excellence. Jim Crawford's spirit prevails, and he would have it no other way."

Southern Polytechnic State University

A UNIVERSITY THAT OFFERS BACHELOR'S AND MASTER'S DEGREE PROGRAMS in the technologies and sciences, Southern Polytechnic State University practices the scholarship of application. Says President Dr. Lisa Rossbacher, "Our philosophy of teaching and our programs are based on involving students in both learning and applying knowledge to create solutions. We believe strongly in the relevance of intellectual and practical education to today's technology-oriented world."

Since its inception, the school has been closely tied to business and industry. Established as the Technical Institute in 1948 at the request of the Georgia Business & Industry Association, it was originally part of the Georgia Institute of Technology (also known as Georgia Tech). In 1970, Southern Polytechnic became a four-year college offering bachelor's degrees, and a decade later, it became independent of Georgia Tech. In 1980, Southern Polytechnic became the 33rd institution in the University System of Georgia.

STUDENTS ARE IN DEMAND

In this age of technology, Southern Polytechnic students are much in demand, and a high percentage are employed in their fields upon graduation. The school has a solid career development and placement program, and has forged close bonds with businesses and industries throughout metro Atlanta and the region. The university's faculty members are attuned to the needs and requirements of the business world; most have a combination of both strong academic credentials and industrial backgrounds, and are actively engaged as consultants in their fields of expertise.

In addition, Southern Polytechnic State University offers extensive opportunities for internships and work-study programs with local businesses, and a large number of students are employed part-time by metro Atlanta companies. Overall, the school works with more than 1,400 companies in co-op, temporary, and permanent placement of its students.

"Our students learn to grow, evolve, and adapt throughout their careers, so they will have the intellectual skills to go from working for a company early in their careers to later running a company," says Rossbacher. While Southern Polytechnic grounds students in the technical side of various science and engineering fields, it also emphasizes critical thinking, problem solving, and clear written and oral communication. "The ability to work effectively in groups and individually and the ability to express one's ideas, no matter how technical, transcend pure academic skills," Rossbacher notes.

Some 4,000 students from 35 states and more than 80 countries pursue degrees at Southern Polytechnic State University, located in Marietta, a historic city just northwest of downtown Atlanta. Through its School of Architecture, College of Arts and Sciences, School of Management, and College of Technology, the university offers master of science degrees, including engineering technology, computer science, software engineering, management, construction, technical and professional communications, and quality assurance. It also offers bachelor of science degrees in nearly 20 fields, ranging from civil engineering technology, architecture, and telecommunications engineering technology—the first and currently only such degree program in Georgia and the Southeast—to construction, manufacturing, and apparel and textile engineering technology. It is the only public university in Georgia offering a five-year, nationally accredited bachelor of architecture degree. In addition, Southern Polytechnic was the first university in Georgia and is one of a small number nationwide to offer a complete degree program via the Internet: the master of science in quality assurance.

Today, Southern Polytechnic State University plays a key role among universities and in business and industry in Georgia and the Southeast. The school produces well-educated graduates who can implement today's technology and effectively lead the science and technology companies of the future.

CLOCKWISE FROM TOP LEFT: SOUTHERN POLYTECHNIC STATE UNIVERSITY'S FACULTY MEMBERS ARE ATTUNED TO THE NEEDS AND REQUIREMENTS OF THE BUSINESS WORLD.

"OUR STUDENTS LEARN TO GROW, EVOLVE, AND ADAPT THROUGHOUT THEIR CAREERS, SO THEY WILL HAVE THE INTELLECTUAL SKILLS TO GO FROM WORKING FOR A COMPANY EARLY IN THEIR CAREERS TO LATER RUNNING A COMPANY," SAYS PRESIDENT DR. LISA ROSSBACHER.

IN THIS AGE OF TECHNOLOGY, SOUTHERN POLYTECHNIC STUDENTS ARE MUCH IN DEMAND, AND A HIGH PERCENTAGE ARE EMPLOYED IN THEIR FIELDS UPON GRADUATION.

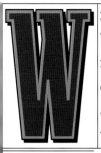 ITH A FLEET OF WIDELY RECOGNIZABLE BROWN VEHICLES AND AIRCRAFT, United Parcel Service (UPS) delivers more than 12 million documents and parcels in more than 200 countries and territories every day, totaling more than 3 billion deliveries every year. These accomplishments truly make UPS the world leader in package distribution, express package delivery, and document delivery.

A STRING OF FIRSTS

Generating nearly $25 billion in annual revenue, UPS is the largest employer based in metro Atlanta. Founded in Seattle in 1907, the company was the dream of 19-year-old Jim Casey, who borrowed $100 from a friend to get his venture going. Dubbed United Parcel Service in 1915, it boasts a litany of firsts in its industry. Among them are the first mechanical sorter and conveyor belt (1926), the world's first air express service (1929), the first package delivery company to gather delivery and pickup information electronically (1991), and the first to offer on-line service for electronic delivery—both audio and visual—of data and documents (1998).

"E-commerce is changing the way we do business, both business-to-business and business-to-consumer," says UPS Chairman and CEO Jim Kelly, who has been with UPS since 1964. More and more, people are conducting trade and relaying information electronically, he notes, adding that the potential for UPS' growth on this front is tremendous. The company spends approximately $1 billion per year on information services and business solutions—a figure that is more than UPS' outlay for physical assets, such as vehicles and buildings. This comparison speaks volumes about the commerce of the future.

A PEOPLE BUSINESS

Through nearly a century of business, UPS has pioneered concepts and services in the delivery industry and has experienced tremendous growth nationally and internationally. For 16 consecutive years, the package delivery giant has been ranked

by *Fortune* magazine as the most admired mail, package, and freight delivery company in America. In 1998 and 1999, the company won that same title on a global scale. "Such recognition is high praise," comments Kelly, "but, like our growth, it is something we could never have achieved without the commitment and hard work of our people."

The total number of employees in the company is nearing 327,000 worldwide. "Even though UPS is a large, global company, we have the ability to adapt and change and provide new solutions for our customers," Kelly says. From delivery options to logistics and supply chain solutions, no other company comes close to UPS' vast coverage and breadth of services.

"And we have built a reputation for reliability. That is because of the dedication of our employees and their commitment to serve customers and do the best possible job." In fact, this attitude is one of the strengths of UPS, according to Kelly, and a quality of which the company is most proud. This dedication has made UPS a leader throughout the 20th century and will carry it on throughout the new millennium.

UNDER THE LEADERSHIP OF UPS CHAIRMAN AND CHIEF EXECUTIVE OFFICER JIM KELLY, THE WORLD'S LARGEST PACKAGE AND EXPRESS DELIVERY COMPANY LOOKS TO CONTINUE ITS FOCUS ON GLOBAL EXPANSION AND ELECTRONIC COMMERCE IN THE NEW MILLENNIUM.

Scientific-Atlanta

THE FUTURE OF TELEVISION, PROMISED FOR SO LONG, IS HERE. FOR A LONG time, television was a place to watch broadcast programs on one of only a few channels. Then came cable, which has many more programming choices, but still provides a passive viewing experience. In the near future, however, viewers will be able to search an interactive on-line guide of hundreds of channels—by channel, time, date, theme, or title. Television programming, Internet access, and e-mail will be totally integrated, allowing viewers to watch a show, click on an on-screen icon to learn more about a related topic or buy a featured item, then e-mail friends. This same technology will also give viewers the ability to fast-forward, pause, and rewind a digital movie or television program at their convenience, just as if they had rented a video or recorded the show—only without a trip to the video store, a DVD player, or a VCR. And that's only the beginning.

Scientific-Atlanta leads the way in bringing more choices, better control, and greater satisfaction to cable TV operators and consumers. Digital services on the company's award-winning Explorer® platform are available from many major U.S. and Canadian cable systems. Scientific-Atlanta's digital networks and set-top converters are all designed to support interactive, two-way applications ranging from video-on-demand to e-commerce to downloading music over the Internet.

MANY OF SCIENTIFIC-ATLANTA'S MOST INNOVATIVE RESEARCH AND DEVELOPMENT EFFORTS TAKE PLACE AT THE COMPANY'S FACILITY ON SUGARLOAF PARKWAY. THE FACILITY COUPLES ITS STATE-OF-THE-ART LABORATORY AND PRESENTATION AND CONFERENCE CENTERS WITH AMENITIES LIKE JOGGING TRAILS, A FULL-SERVICE CAFETERIA, COURTYARDS, AND A SOON-TO-BE-COMPLETED BALL FIELD AND INDOOR FITNESS CENTER.

A HISTORY OF VISION AND LEADERSHIP

Scientific-Atlanta was founded in 1951 by seven Georgia Institute of Technology engineer-entrepreneurs to manufacture electronics products, mostly for the defense industry. In 1966, just a few years after the birth of the cable industry, the company began manufacturing products for cable operators. From there, the company pioneered a long string of firsts,

including applications that tracked the first successful U.S. space flight; the first live satellite-to-cable transmissions, necessary for cable systems to carry more than just local programming; the first live international satellite transmission (the Thrilla in Manila heavyweight title fight between Muhammad Ali and Joe Frazier); and the first live programming to a naval vessel at sea (the 1998 Super Bowl). The company has since grown to be a $1.2 billion firm with more than 6,200 employees around the world.

Scientific-Atlanta's early recognition of the importance and potential of cable telecommunications and its visionary emphasis on digital interactive network technology has led to the company's current position as an industry leader. In a world where people want sophisticated on-line capabilities delivered with tremendous ease of use, Scientific-Atlanta brings the possibilities of global digital entertainment and information and the connectivity of worldwide networking right to viewers' television sets.

POISED TO SUCCEED IN A WORLD OF CONVERGENCE

There is little doubt that the worlds of computers, telecommunications, and cable television are converging to make all kinds of new services possible for consumers. The Internet has dramatically changed what people can do with their PCs and televisions. People increasingly want to communicate, find information, make purchases, and be entertained in a real-time, interactive environment. They want that environment to be exciting to look at, with compelling graphics, great sound and full motion, and digital video.

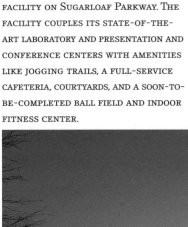

At the same time, many people are intimidated by the costs and learning curve associated with even the most user-friendly PCs. Scientific-Atlanta bridges the gap with solutions that help operators deliver the services people want over their central source of information and entertainment, the television set. These solutions include the video compression systems that deliver the programming to cable operators, the fiber-optic and coaxial cable-based broadband access systems that distribute content to end users, and the set-tops and systems that let consumers receive content on their televisions. As President and CEO Jim McDonald says, "We, more than anyone else, have the end-to-end technology and system solutions necessary to deliver advanced digital interactive services to consumers."

Scientific-Atlanta solutions extend beyond cable operators, as well, with satellite solutions that provide advanced video compression capabilities.

A VITAL FORCE IN THE ATLANTA COMMUNITY

Scientific-Atlanta continues to grow and prosper because of its commitment to innovation and integrity. The company attracts outstanding talent from around the world and supports them with top research and development labs and a challenge to create the technology that will deliver the future of telecommunications. The beneficiaries are consumers and Scientific-Atlanta's customers, including leading cable operators around the world, such as Time Warner, AT&T BIS, Cox Communications, Comcast, Charter Communications, and Adelphia Cable. The company's customers also include several of the world's most prominent broadcasters and programmers, such as ESPN, Toon Disney, CNN, and Discovery Channel, as well as service providers, such as PanAmSat, Hong Kong Telecom, and ARABSAT.

As a leader within the Atlanta business community, Scientific-Atlanta takes its responsibility as a corporate citizen seriously. The company invests both time and business dollars in a planned, consistent manner to make a difference in the community where so many of its employees work and live. When the Olympic Games came to Atlanta in 1996, Scientific-Atlanta was there as a major sponsor, providing Olympic administrators and the media with simultaneous coverage of all televised Olympic Games activity.

The company also supports numerous cultural and civic programs throughout the year. Senior managers often take leadership roles in community projects and serve on nonprofit boards. A large percentage of Scientific-Atlanta employees also participate in company-sponsored volunteer efforts. Additionally, donations made through the Scientific-Atlanta Foundation have made it one of the top charitable contributors in the Atlanta area, according to the Atlanta Foundations Center.

Far from resting on past accomplishments, the company continues to maintain a forward-thinking focus. "Now is the time to move ahead," says McDonald, "by really listening to and understanding what our customers need, and delivering the support, services, and applications that will create new opportunities in the future."

INTERNET ACCESS OVER THE TELEVISION SET IS A REALITY FOR ELEMENTARY SCHOOL TEACHER RUTH JOHNSON AND HER SON, EARL, USING SCIENTIFIC-ATLANTA'S 8600^{XTM} ADVANCED ANALOG SET-TOPS.

SCIENTIFIC-ATLANTA'S EXPLORER 2000 SET-TOP AND APPLICATIONS CREATE A CONVENIENT, ENJOYABLE VIEWING EXPERIENCE FOR PEOPLE NATIONWIDE, LIKE THE CARDUCCI FAMILY, CUSTOMERS OF TIME WARNER CABLE IN THE TAMPA BAY AREA.

ACH YEAR, BASS HOTELS & RESORTS HOSTS MORE THAN 150 MILLION GUESTS at its more than 2,800 hotels located in some 90 countries and territories throughout the Americas, Africa, Asia, Europe, the Pacific Rim, and the Middle East. Bass Hotels & Resorts properties, both franchised and company-owned, are among the most familiar names in lodging in the world: Inter-Continental, Crowne Plaza, Holiday Inn, Holiday Inn Express, and Staybridge Suites by Holiday Inn.

With some operations headquartered in Atlanta, Bass Hotels & Resorts is the hotel business of London-based Bass PLC, a global leader in pubs, restaurants, and branded drinks, including Carling, the UK's top consumer brand of beer; Tennent's Lager; Grolsch; and the venerable Bass Ale.

A DECADE OF CHANGE AND MOMENTUM

The 1990s was a monumental decade for Bass Hotels & Resorts. Bass PLC acquired the Holiday Inn chain in 1990, and the following year moved the chain's headquarters from Memphis to metro Atlanta. According to Chairman and CEO Thomas R. Oliver, the company set a goal to become a global leader in the lodging business, and Atlanta offered worldwide transportation access, a broad corporate infrastructure, and an international presence and recognition.

The company embarked on a huge capital investment program of $750 million a year for both acquisitions and renovation, and undertook an ambitious program to modernize and freshen its properties and to expand its menu of brands. One of the first steps was the introduction of Holiday Inn Express for the limited-service/midmarket category, appealing to both business and leisure travelers. The brand has been tremendously successful and has opened more than 100 locations a year worldwide since 1993.

In 1994, Bass Hotels & Resorts developed Crowne Plaza's image as a separate brand to reflect its upscale market appeal, and in 1997, launched Staybridge Suites by Holiday Inn in the extended-stay market. The first Staybridge Suites hotel opened in north metro Atlanta in 1998, and the company has projected that it will have more than 200 Staybridge Suites—about 50 company-owned and 150 franchises—by 2002.

In 1998, Bass acquired Inter-Continental Hotels and Resorts, a $2.9 billion deal that essentially put Bass Hotels & Resorts on the first-class hotel map around the

ESTABLISHED IN MEMPHIS IN 1952, THE HOLIDAY INN BRAND—ACQUIRED IN 1990 BY BASS HOTELS & RESORTS' PARENT COMPANY, BASS PLC—COULD BE FOUND IN CITIES AND TOWNS AROUND THE WORLD. COMMENTS KEMMONS WILSON, FOUNDER, WHO IS STILL INVOLVED IN THE HOLIDAY INN HOTEL BUSINESS, "IT'S UNBELIEVABLE THE WAY IT HAS KEPT ON GROWING."

BASS HOTELS & RESORTS IS COMMITTED TO BUILDING AND DEVELOPING BRANDS OUTSIDE THE UNITED STATES, SUCH AS THE HOLIDAY INN MIRI IN SARAWAK, MALAYSIA, AND THE AMSTEL INTER-CONTINENTAL IN AMSTERDAM.

world. For some 50 years, Inter-Continental has been one of the most recognized high-end international hotel names, with operations in 73 countries. The purchase gave Bass Hotels & Resorts the distinction of being the most geographically diverse lodging company in the world.

GLOBAL ASPIRATIONS

Thomas R. Oliver joined Bass Hotels & Resorts in 1997, and is experienced in global operations from years of service at Federal Express in Worldwide Customer Operations and from 15 years in executive positions with Thomas Cook, Inc. and American Airlines. When he joined the company, 80 percent of Bass Hotels & Resorts' revenues came from U.S. operations. By 1999, with increased international business and the acquisition of Inter-Continental, 53 percent of revenues were from the United States. "We are committed to building and developing brands outside the United States to the same level of significance that we reached in this country," says Oliver. By 2004, Bass plans to add more than 1,200 properties worldwide among its various brands.

Bass Hotels & Resorts is the largest operating unit of Bass PLC, but until 1998, it represented only about 25 percent of its parent company's operating profits. That year, the percentage jumped to 40 percent and has increased annually.

SWINGS AND CYCLES

The hospitality industry is fraught with swings and cycles based on a number of factors. The growth of the gross national product, an aging population with more time for leisure, an increase in per capita income, and a desire to travel on the part of an increasingly sophisticated population all factor into Bass Hotels & Resorts' projection for a more than 3 percent per annum increase in hotel room demand for the next 20-plus years.

Bass Hotels & Resorts has made a point of covering all markets,

from value-priced to luxury accommodations. This array of brands and price levels will keep the company growing. Internationally, there are hot spots of growth at various times. "We look for indications of growth before the fact," Oliver notes, "so that we are ready with product when the time is ripe."

Atlanta, for example, has been a significant market, and Bass Hotels & Resorts has introduced at least two concepts in the metro market. One of the newest is the Holiday Inn of the Future. The company broke ground for its first property near the Atlanta airport in 1999. The hotel features a residential feel and a full array of electronic services.

Holiday Inn founder Kemmons Wilson never imagined what would develop when he opened his first hotel in Memphis in 1952. After opening the facility, with its basic concept of family- and value-oriented service, Wilson became a pioneer in the franchising business, and rapidly expanded the Holiday Inn system along interstates across the United

States. By the end of the 1980s, the Holiday Inn brand could be found in cities and towns around the world. Comments the octogenarian, who is still involved in the Holiday Inn hotel business, "It's unbelievable the way it has kept on growing." To which Oliver adds, "We think that when he turns 100, he will still have good reason to say that."

AS PART OF AN AMBITIOUS PROGRAM TO MODERNIZE AND FRESHEN ITS PROPERTIES, BASS HOTELS & RESORTS INTRODUCED HOLIDAY INN EXPRESS IN 1993 FOR THE LIMITED-SERVICE/MIDMARKET CATEGORY, APPEALING TO BOTH BUSINESS AND LEISURE TRAVELERS. THE BRAND HAS BEEN TREMENDOUSLY SUCCESSFUL AND HAS OPENED MORE THAN 100 LOCATIONS A YEAR WORLDWIDE (TOP).

IN 1994, BASS HOTELS & RESORTS DEVELOPED CROWNE PLAZA'S IMAGE AS A SEPARATE BRAND TO REFLECT ITS UPSCALE MARKET APPEAL (BOTTOM).

Waffle House, Inc.

MORE THAN 200 BRIGHT YELLOW SIGNS MARK THE LOCATIONS OF WAFFLE House restaurants along city streets and interstate highways around metro Atlanta. Waffle House is a homegrown Atlanta institution that offers a combination of Good Food Fast®, as its motto states, and outstanding service. Since the first restaurant opened Labor Day 1955 in Avondale Estates, GA, a suburb of Atlanta, the company has grown

to include more than 1,200 restaurants in 24 states—primarily in the Southeast, but also as far north as Maryland and as far west as Arizona.

ANY TIME, ANY DAY

According to its slogan, Waffle House is America's Place to Eat®. If people have a hankering for grits, hashbrowns, waffles, cheese 'n eggs, hamburgers, or T-bone steaks, they can get it at their nearest Waffle House 24 hours a day, 365 days a year. Cooking up breakfast, lunch, and dinner at any hour, this southern icon prides itself on welcoming and serving America.

In Atlanta, the restaurant chain is consistently voted the city's favorite after-2 a.m. stop. But at virtually any time—day or night—construction workers, families, teenagers, retirees, sports celebrities, politicians, and suited business executives are perched at the counter or seated in a booth. What really sets Waffle House apart is the unique dining experience that customers receive. The

kitchen is out in front and in full view. Regulars are greeted by name and enjoy the social interaction with their servers and other customers. All food is prepared fresh, cooked to order, and served on real china, with consistent quality from location to location. At Waffle House, customers enjoy sit-down table service with the speed of delivery typically found at fast-food establishments.

Coffee is the restaurant's bestseller; Waffle House serves more than 80 million cups each year. Second on the list are the legendary hashbrowns, which can be ordered with any combination of the following: scattered, smothered, covered, chunked, topped, diced, or peppered (translation: scattered on the grill, smothered with onions, covered with cheese, chunked with ham, topped with chili, diced with tomatoes, or

CLOCKWISE FROM TOP:
THE DISTINCTIVE BUILDING DESIGN AND BIG YELLOW SIGN HAVE BECOME FAMILIAR SIGHTS ALONG INTERSTATE HIGHWAYS AND CITY STREETS.

THE WAFFLE HOUSE MENU FEATURES SIGNATURE MEALS ALONG WITH AMERICA'S BEST BRANDS. THE WAFFLE HOUSE DOORS ARE OPEN 24 HOURS A DAY, 365 DAYS A YEAR.

ALL MEALS ARE COOKED TO ORDER, PREPARED RIGHT IN FRONT OF THE CUSTOMERS' EYES.

peppered with green chile peppers). Of course, another Waffle House favorite is the World Famous Waffle, served up plain or with pecans. Since opening in 1955, Waffle House has served over 350 million orders of waffles, validating its claim as World's Leading Server. Waffle House is also the world's leading server of hashbrowns, omelets, cheese 'n eggs, raisin toast, grits, steak and eggs, apple butter, T-bone steaks, pork chops, country ham, patty melts, and USDA choice hamburgers.

A PEOPLE BUSINESS

Waffle House is truly a people-driven business. When neighbors Joe Rogers Jr. and Tom Forkner opened the first Waffle House, they wanted to create a company that served folks on both sides of the counter—customers and associates. Waffle House, Inc. is now headed by the cofounder's son, Joe Rogers Jr., who began busing tables as a youngster and became president in 1973. Rogers continues the emphasis on people that was established at the outset, and he spends the majority of his time out among the restaurants.

Waffle House, Inc. is employee-owned and owner-managed. Both hourly and management associates are able to buy stock in the company. Happily for those stockhold-

ers, Waffle House has performed well and continues to grow and succeed—helping the restaurant live by its claim as America's Place to Work®. In fact, there are countless success stories of associates who have built their careers with Waffle House and accumulated a substantial stock nest egg. As the company tells its associates, "Our future, including the growth of Waffle House stock, is what we make of it—each of us can make a big difference in building sales and controlling costs."

While employee ownership may not be unusual in other industries, it is rare in the food service business, as are the health benefits provided by Waffle House, Inc. These opportunities, combined with incentive-based compensation and bonuses, make Waffle House an attractive long-term career choice where associates have a vested interest in the company's success.

WAFFLE DOO WOP

The restaurant is cooking up more than just good food. Waffle House, whose jukeboxes are as much a part of the ambience as the yellow signs, has a musical listing all its own. Inside the restaurants, customers can tap their forks and spoons to any one of the classic waffle songs, such as "Waffle Doo Wop," "Good Food Fast," and "Waffle House Family." And these specially written songs can be taken home on the company's first CD, *Waffle House Jukebox Favorites: Volume I*.

On a typical day at a local Waffle House location, the bright yellow sign greets each customer like an old friend, the jukebox hums a familiar Waffle House tune, and the staff makes everyone who enters the door feel right at home. Whether it's waffles and hashbrowns or the "Waffle Doo Wop," there's always something cooking at Waffle House.

PEOPLE COME TO WAFFLE HOUSE FOR GOOD FOOD FAST, FRIENDLY SERVICE, AND GREAT VALUE (TOP).

SINCE 1955, THE UNIQUE WAFFLE HOUSE EXPERIENCE HAS MADE IT A BELOVED ICON OF THE SOUTH (BOTTOM).

Cathedral of the Holy Spirit

A FAMILIAR METRO-AREA LANDMARK, THE SPIRE ATOP THE CATHEDRAL OF THE Holy Spirit pierces the Atlanta skyline. The fan-shaped, neo-Gothic structure is the center of an expanding east Atlanta complex the Cathedral at Chapel Hill, established in 1960. Serving a local congregation of thousands of members, this interdenominational church encompasses worship, education, recreation, the arts, television

and audio and video recording.

Cofounder Archbishop Earl Paulk Jr. is the creator of a far-reaching mission he describes as One Blood. The phrase that defines the work of the Cathedral at Chapel Hill is taken from Acts 17:24-28, spoken by the apostle Paul: "And he hath made from one blood every nation of men to dwell on all the face of the earth."

Paulk interprets that message to mean that all people, no matter their ethnic background or skin color, are equal and of one origin. He; his wife, Norma; his brother, Don Paulk; and Don's wife, Clariece, are striving to make this belief a reality. Since the first church's formation near downtown Atlanta in 1960, they have brought together people from diverse races and socioeconomic levels to establish one of the first truly integrated churches in the area.

MAKING IT UP TO SAMMY

T he calling to ministry went back two generations in the Paulk family, and Earl Paulk, Jr. followed those footsteps beginning at age 17. But the incident

that set him on the path toward his mission happened on his uncle's south Georgia farm. Eleven-year-old Earl, visiting for the summer, befriended a black teenage field-worker named Sammy. One day, while he was plowing, Sammy did not follow instructions closely, and in a fit of anger, the uncle shot him with buckshot. Shocked and horrified, Paulk wept as he washed blood from his friend's back. "All I could say at the time was, 'I'll make this up to you someday,

Sammy,' " says Paulk.

Paulk has spent a lifetime keeping his promise. In the early 1950s, even as he attended Candler School of Theology at Emory University, he began to confront racial inequities. Since then, Paulk has been on the front lines of integration efforts throughout the Atlanta area. He worked with Martin Luther King Sr., Martin Luther King Jr., Andrew Young, and others during the civil rights years, and has continued the fight

CLOCKWISE FROM TOP:
THE CATHEDRAL OF THE HOLY SPIRIT IS ONE OF ATLANTA'S LARGEST HOUSES OF WORSHIP.

THOUSANDS OF ATLANTANS GATHER EACH SUNDAY MORNING FOR WORSHIP IN THE NEO-GOTHIC-STYLE CATHEDRAL, WHICH ENCOMPASSES MORE THAN 160,000 SQUARE FEET AND SITS ON MORE THAN 120 ACRES OF LAND.

THE CATHEDRAL IS KNOWN AROUND THE WORLD THROUGH ITS INTERNATIONAL TELEVISION PROGRAM, *THE CATHEDRAL AT CHAPEL HILL*. THE CATHEDRAL CHOIR, ORCHESTRA, AND SINGERS MINISTER TO MILLIONS WEEKLY WITH A VARIETY OF MUSIC.

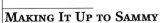

to break down racial and social barriers.

A RECOGNITION OF HUMAN NEEDS

Although we attend to spiritual needs, we strongly believe that each of us has a job to do here on Earth," says Paulk. For the founding pastors, that job includes a unique social responsibility. "Our theology is that the power of the Holy Spirit is at work charismatically through works of human hands. We are ecumenical human beings," Paulk says.

Putting that theology into practice, the Paulks and fellow believers have established programs to address the needs of the community. "Every person should have a chance to become the best he or she can be through education, the arts, sports, or whatever means possible," says Paulk. The Cathedral of the Holy Spirit operates the Earl Paulk Institute, a Bible school offering both associate's and bachelor's degrees in theology, human services, and practical and applied ministry; Cathedral Academy for kindergarten through 12th grade; and continuing education courses for pastors, congregation members, and the community.

To help maintain integration, the Cathedral has bought surrounding acreage and leased it to builders in the church. Four subdivisions of mixed-income, single-family homes and condominiums have been built near the Cathedral complex. All are fully integrated.

The church began an outreach program in 1989 with Operation Dignity, a model in U.S. cities as well as in other countries. Partnering with public housing communities and drawing on the support of its own members and local organizations, the Cathedral adopts residents of troubled neighborhoods, offering literacy programs for children and adults, recreational and arts programs, building, job training, and, says Paulk, "above all, hope." Its first effort with Bankhead Courts, then one of Atlanta's most dangerous and drug-ridden areas, won a Point of Light Award from former President George Bush. The Cathedral continues to extend its efforts to other Atlanta neighborhoods as well.

The multicultural congregation is evident in the church's choir, orchestra, and various musical groups, including its spirited Firebrand Youth Choir. Classical concert pianist Pastor Clariece Paulk directs the worship and arts department, and has been instrumental in making music, dance, and theater an integral part of programs for worship services and community presentations, as well as audiovisual recordings. The music and dance performed by the Cathedral groups encompass familiar hymns and gospel, rock, and classical music. Dance and music conservatories help to enhance the lives of children and adults within the church and community. Visual arts are equally important, and the murals, paintings, and woodwork in the Cathedral of the Holy Spirit were designed and painted by members of the congregation.

"We are challenged to be a 21st-century-model church," says Paulk. He believes it is the church's responsibility to demonstrate that all can live together in peace and unity. "We can solve the problems of disharmony through communication and a true acceptance of human worth," adds Paulk.

Paulk also contends that churches must break down barriers between denominations and work together for the good of the community and for peace in the future. "Why would we not?" he asks.

BISHOP EARL PAULK, FOUNDER OF THE CATHEDRAL AT CHAPEL HILL; HIS BROTHER, PASTOR DON PAULK; AND THEIR WIVES HAVE BEEN MINISTERING IN ATLANTA FOR MORE THAN 50 YEARS (TOP).

KNOWN FOR THEIR INNOVATIVE STYLE OF WORSHIP, THE CATHEDRAL DANCERS MINISTER IN DANCE EACH WEEK. HUNDREDS OF CHILDREN ARE INVOLVED DAILY IN THE CATHEDRAL'S MUSIC AND DANCE CONSERVATORIES (BOTTOM).

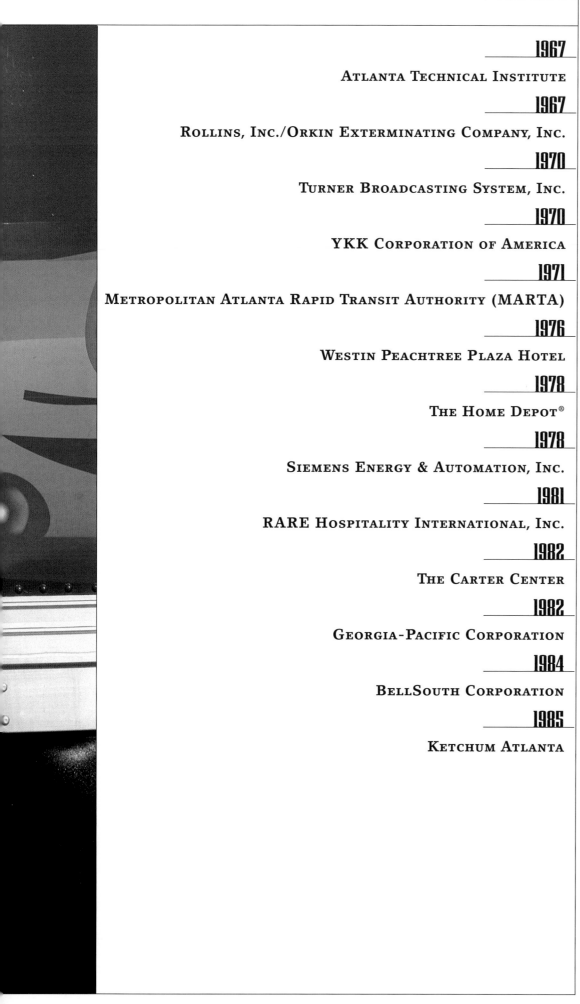

1967

ATLANTA TECHNICAL INSTITUTE

1967

ROLLINS, INC./ORKIN EXTERMINATING COMPANY, INC.

1970

TURNER BROADCASTING SYSTEM, INC.

1970

YKK CORPORATION OF AMERICA

1971

METROPOLITAN ATLANTA RAPID TRANSIT AUTHORITY (MARTA)

1976

WESTIN PEACHTREE PLAZA HOTEL

1978

THE HOME DEPOT®

1978

SIEMENS ENERGY & AUTOMATION, INC.

1981

RARE HOSPITALITY INTERNATIONAL, INC.

1982

THE CARTER CENTER

1982

GEORGIA-PACIFIC CORPORATION

1984

BELLSOUTH CORPORATION

1985

KETCHUM ATLANTA

© BUD LEE

Atlanta Technical Institute

AS IT ENTERS THE NEW MILLENNIUM, ATLANTA TECHNICAL INSTITUTE IS experiencing an era of explosive growth in both its programs and its facilities. "These are exciting times for the school," says Dr. Brenda Watts Jones, president of Atlanta Tech. "Our growth is unprecedented, and we are on a new path to build an unbeatable reputation for providing the best-quality technical training." ❏ Jones initially joined

DR. BRENDA WATTS JONES, PRESIDENT OF ATLANTA TECHNICAL INSTITUTE, WAS THE FIRST AFRICAN-AMERICAN WOMAN TO BE NAMED PRESIDENT OF A GEORGIA TECHNICAL SCHOOL (TOP).

AS IT ENTERS THE NEW MILLENNIUM, ATLANTA TECH IS EXPERIENCING AN ERA OF EXPLOSIVE GROWTH IN BOTH ITS PROGRAMS AND ITS FACILITIES (BOTTOM).

Atlanta Tech to guide the school through a major transition. Founded as a vocational school in 1945, it had been under the auspices of the City of Atlanta Board of Education public school system. In 1997, Atlanta Tech took its place as a member of Georgia's network of 33 postsecondary technical institutes under the Georgia Department of Technical and Adult Education. On July 1 that same year, Jones was offered the presidency of Atlanta Tech and became the first African-American woman to be named president of a Georgia technical school.

Since that milestone year for Atlanta Tech, enrollment in the two-year institution has jumped nearly 20 percent annually to more than 4,000 students. There's little slowdown in sight, as demand for qualified, technically trained employees continues to grow in the Southeast. Atlanta Tech serves

Fulton County, south of the Chattahoochee River, and while the majority of the school's students are residents of the county, there are an increasing number from other areas of Georgia, as well as a notable growth in international enrollees.

CURTIS COMPTON PHOTOGRAPHY

GUARANTEED SKILLS

Our location dictates our mission," says Jones. Atlanta Tech is in the Southeast, which has enjoyed an expanding economy and is surrounded in metro Atlanta with a large base of Fortune 500 companies, a huge visitor and hospitality market, and a burgeoning high-tech industry. "Our mission is to provide quality technical training through a technology-based vocational education curriculum, and our goal is to offer the very best in technical education in the region," asserts Jones.

Like its sister schools in the network, Atlanta Tech offers a guarantee to both its students and their employers. "We guarantee our product," says Jones, who tells companies, "If we train someone and an employer is not satisfied, we will retrain that employee at no cost to either the student or the company. We intend to give you what you want."

Atlanta Tech's strength is its ability to produce quality students with sound technical skills that address the needs of metro Atlanta business and industry. The school's programs reflect the diverse economy of the area, offering more than 45 diploma and short-term programs and additional continuing education programs. Among the broad range of programs of study are aviation, electronics, practical nursing, cosmetology, automotive collision repair, medical laboratory technology, dental assisting, and culinary arts. The most popular programs are computer technology, allied health, cosmetology, and aviation/avionics.

Since 1997, Atlanta Tech has added more than 20 new diploma and short programs, including

RON WITHERSPOON PHOTOGRAPHY

JONES (THIRD FROM LEFT), GEORGIA GOVERNOR ROY BARNES, AND OTHER SUPPORTERS OF ATLANTA TECHNICAL INSTITUTE SHARE IN THE CUTTING OF THE RIBBON AND THE EXCITEMENT OF THE SCHOOL'S NEW MAIN ENTRANCE.

paramedic training, certified nursing assistance, and fiber optics technology. In late 1999, the school completed a new, $1.3 million campus renovation.

TRAINING ATLANTA'S WORKFORCE

Not all classes are held on Atlanta Tech's main campus. Hartsfield Atlanta International Airport and the hangar and facilities of the airport's largest tenant, Delta Air Lines, are also classrooms. Aviation and avionics are popular courses of study specifically because the school has partnered with these leading entities to train students on-site.

The school and the Atlanta airport have teamed up to offer training to all airport employees— some 38,000 each quarter. Atlanta Tech also has partnerships with Fulton County, AT&T, Hyatt Hotels, Atlanta Public Schools, J.B. Hunt, and the City of Atlanta Fire Department, as well as a local carpenters' union for construction education. Jones is aggressively seeking new partnerships with business and industry in and around Atlanta. "I say to CEOs and other municipal and company leaders, 'We are training your workforce,' " says Jones. "How better to do so than to have the company involved in the process?"

The school is also working closely with the Department of Technical and Adult Education's Quick Start program, a statewide, comprehensive training program designed to meet a company's specific workforce needs. The shortage of skilled workers in the Atlanta area is driving the success of this program. The corporation's needs are assessed, and education developmental specialists determine the performance requirements and appropriate training. They design a training plan for that corporation, including specific job tasks, related skills, and technology training, along with leadership and work culture development. "We work closely with the companies to understand their business and what they need from their employees," notes Jones.

FACILITIES FOR THE MILLENNIUM

Reflecting the expansion in programs and Jones' drive to make Atlanta Technical Institute a key player in a city known for business and industry, the school has undertaken its first major renovation and building project since the 1970s. It includes modernizing classrooms, an interior and exterior face-lift, and a new main entrance. Phase II is already in the works, with plans for a new administrative area, a center for economic development, and a three-story allied health building on campus. Jones also hopes to add two more buildings with state-of-the-art equipment and classrooms. As need dictates, Atlanta Tech expects to establish satellite facilities in the future.

The institution considers all of metro Atlanta its market, and a great number of metro Atlanta companies—from multibillion-dollar corporations to entrepreneurial ventures—have a need for well-trained employees. Jones is determined to see that Atlanta Technical Institute provides them.

Rollins, Inc./Orkin Exterminating Company, Inc.

FOR MORE THAN 50 YEARS, ONE CORPORATE NAME HAS BEEN SYNONYMOUS with quality consumer services–Rollins, Inc. Recognized by *Forbes* magazine as the Nation's Number One Service Company for eight consecutive years, Rollins has grown from its inception as a radio and television broadcasting company to become one of the nation's largest consumer services organizations. A pioneer in such consumer services as wireless residential security systems, cable television, outdoor advertising, and pest control, Rollins' core business of pest control extends today throughout the United States, Mexico, Canada, and the Caribbean under the widely recognized name of its wholly owned subsidiary, Orkin Exterminating Company, Inc.

A Rich History

The history of Rollins begins with the company's founder, O. Wayne Rollins. Born in the north Georgia mountains near the town of Ringgold, Wayne and his brother, John W. Rollins, grew up on the family farm. They worked as farmers, laborers, and entrepreneurs, and in 1948, they formed a business partnership that was the beginning of Rollins, Inc. John operated automobile dealerships in Delaware and Maryland, while Wayne opened their first radio station in Virginia. As he acquired more radio stations in other markets, Wayne became one of the first in radio broadcasting history to tailor programming to specific community segments–a practice known today as niche marketing.

From their success in radio broadcasting, the Rollins brothers entered the television industry in 1956. Rollins Broadcasting of Wilmington, Delaware, went public in 1960 and was listed on the Nasdaq exchange. The next year, Rollins' stock began trading on the American Stock Exchange. In 1964, Wayne Rollins made a move that captured the imagination of Wall Street: He purchased Orkin for $62.4 million, nearly seven times Rollins' revenues of $9.1 million. It was the first recorded leveraged buyout in U.S. business history, a transaction that *Business Week* compared to "Jonah swallowing the whale."

The purchase of Orkin was a major turning point in the development of Rollins, Inc., and its corporate history would not be complete without the Orkin story. The pest control company was founded in 1901 by Otto Orkin, a Latvian immigrant, who sold phosphorous paste for rat and roach control door-to-door in Pennsylvania. By 1912, Orkin had moved the growing company to Richmond, Virginia, and added rodent and pest control services. During the 1920s, the company branched out into fumigation and termite control, and Orkin opened his first branch in Atlanta in 1926.

World War II proved a turning point for Orkin, when pest control was declared a necessary service, and the company provided pest control and fumigation for as many as 150 military facilities. The war also pushed forward the development of pest control technology, with Orkin leading the industry by using cutting-edge techniques. After the war, the company expanded rapidly throughout the South, Midwest, and West to become a truly national corporation. Indeed, Orkin built such an extensive empire that *Fortune* magazine once described him as "the General Motors of exterminating."

Rollins' acquisition of the exterminating company in 1964 marked the end of the Otto Orkin era, but not the end of one of America's most familiar advertising icons: the Orkin Man. Once a

CLOCKWISE FROM TOP:
ROLLINS, INC.'S HOME OFFICE IS LOCATED IN ATLANTA.

ON SEPTEMBER 1, 1964, O. WAYNE ROLLINS SIGNED THE CHECK FOR THE PURCHASE OF ORKIN.

IN THE EARLY 1900S, HORSE-DRAWN WAGONS BROUGHT THE ORKIN MAN TO THE HOMES AND BUSINESSES IN ALLENTOWN, PENNSYLVANIA, OFFERING QUALITY PEST CONTROL SERVICES.

cartoon drawing named Otto, it evolved over the years to an all-American television star, animated by sophisticated computer graphics. Today, the Orkin Man is recognized by three out of four Americans, a symbol of the quality and superior service it represents.

In 1967, three years after purchasing Orkin, Rollins moved its headquarters from Delaware to its current location in Atlanta. The company's stock began trading on the New York Stock Exchange the following year. Wayne's sons, R. Randall Rollins and Gary W. Rollins, have had leading roles in the company since 1975 and 1978, respectively. And since the Orkin acquisition more than three decades ago, Rollins has increased its customer base by more than 400 percent, serving more than 1.6 million residential, commercial, and agribusiness customers.

A Leader in the Industry

As one of the largest companies in the exterminating business, Orkin has developed a reputation as a leader in the industry. The company is known for its professionalism, safe practices, and trustworthiness. It is a leader in the development of environmentally friendly materials and procedures, research, and technical training. Working extensively with universities like Texas A&M and Purdue, Orkin has developed rigorous training programs for its technicians, as well as courses in entomology and advanced application techniques.

Rollins is also the permanent sponsor of the O. Orkin Insect Zoo at the National Museum of Natural History at the Smithsonian Institution in Washington, D.C., which studies insects and promotes a better understanding of insects in all environments. To spread the information about good bugs, Rollins provides educational materials for teachers and classrooms, as well as home and business owners. Orkin employees regularly visit schools in local communities to help children and their parents learn about insects.

After three quarters of a century, the enduring image of the Orkin Man still symbolizes the consistent, quality service that is the hallmark of Rollins, Inc.

"I believe our employees have always understood the importance of quality service," says Gary W. Rollins, president and chief operating officer of Rollins, Inc. "Our ongoing educational commitment and pledge to progressive service programs are the keys to our company's future success. Orkin and Rollins employees are smart, professional, and knowledgeable about what they do.

"We, as a company, have changed dramatically over the past five decades," Rollins continues. "When a relatively small broadcasting company purchased Orkin, there may have been skeptics. We have no doubt proved them wrong with the great success we have had in building Orkin into the world's best pest control company."

ROLLINS IS THE PERMANENT SPONSOR OF THE O. ORKIN INSECT ZOO AT THE NATIONAL MUSEUM OF NATURAL HISTORY AT THE SMITHSONIAN INSTITUTE IN WASHINGTON, D.C.

TODAY, ROLLINS IS UNDER THE LEADERSHIP OF FOUNDER O. WAYNE ROLLINS' SONS, CHAIRMAN R. RANDALL ROLLINS (LEFT) AND PRESIDENT GARY W. ROLLINS.

Turner Broadcasting System, Inc.

IT BEGAN SMALL—AND AGAINST ENORMOUS ODDS. IN 1970, R.E. "TED" Turner bought a little, independent Atlanta UHF station, Channel 17. He dubbed it WTCG, and began featuring reruns and wrestling. Six years later, with selected acquisitions under his belt and an expanding audience of viewers, the upstart maverick in the television industry proclaimed his station SuperStation TBS (now TBS Superstation) and sent it to cable systems across the country via satellite. It was the first cable superstation. Early on, the station won the highest ratings for a cable network, and it has held on to that position ever since.

IN 1980, R.E. "TED" TURNER (TOP)— VICE CHAIRMAN OF TIME WARNER, WHICH MERGED WITH TURNER BROAD- CASTING SYSTEM, INC. IN 1996— REVOLUTIONIZED THE BROADCASTING INDUSTRY BY INTRODUCING CABLE NEWS NETWORK (CNN), A 24-HOUR, ALL-NEWS NETWORK (BOTTOM).

A BROADCASTING REVOLUTIONARY

While the other networks had taken notice of this cable network company, renamed Turner Broadcasting System, Inc. (TBS), it was the launching of Cable News Network (CNN) on June 1, 1980, that made them gape. They were witnessing the work of a revolutionary who forever changed television news broadcasting. CNN premiered at 6 p.m. that day, beginning the first 24-hour, all-news network. What's more, it began with 1.7 million subscribers. "It was really a defining moment for Ted Turner, for the company, and for television," says Terence McGuirk, chairman and CEO of TBS, who joined the company in 1972 as an account executive of WTCG. "CNN virtually redefined the concept of television news by giving viewers unprecedented access to history as it happens—anywhere in the world. Today, there's no question that CNN is synonymous with news."

MARK HILL

The addition of CNN Headline News, CNN International (launched in 1985 for viewers outside the United States), and CNNRadio cemented the company's leadership in news coverage worldwide. Four years after its inception, CNN won its first Peabody Award for Excellence in Programming. The company has gone on to capture a number of prestigious Peabody awards, Emmys, Cable Ace awards, and other accolades for its networks and programming, as has its founder, Turner, who graced the cover of *Time* magazine as Man of the Year in 1991.

TURNER BOOSTS MAJOR-LEAGUE SPORTS

Even while still a start-up company, TBS diversified in 1976 when it bought the Atlanta Braves Major League Baseball franchise. A year later, Turner added basketball to the company's sports stable with the purchase of the National Basketball Association's Atlanta Hawks. In 1999, the company brought hockey back to Atlanta with the purchase of a National Hockey League franchise, naming the new team the Atlanta Thrashers after the Georgia state bird.

Atlanta now has Turner Field, affectionately referred to locally as The Ted. Originally known as Olympic Stadium, it hosted the 1996 Centennial Olympic Games, and when it became the home of the Braves, the stadium was named for Turner, who supported major-league sports in Atlanta even through the down years of the

KYLE CHRISTY

Atlanta Braves, before the team won its first National League pennant in 1991. The Hawks and the Thrashers also have a new home, which opened in fall 1999. In an alliance with Royal Philips Electronics of the Netherlands, TBS developed Philips Arena, a 20,000-seat sports facility, adjacent to CNN Center on the site of the Hawks' old arena, the Omni Coliseum.

VISIONS AND MORE REVOLUTIONS

TBS has expanded broadly, driven by Turner's vision and his willingness to try new endeavors in the world of television. Among the various ventures have been the acquisitions of the MGM, pre-1950 Warner Brothers, and RKO film libraries, which include more than 3,000 feature films. TBS debuted Turner Network Television (TNT) in 1988 to 17 million cable homes, the largest network launch to date in cable history. (TNT currently has more than 77 million subscribers.) In keeping with Turner's love of Atlanta and the South, TNT presented the first cable-exclusive telecast of the classic *Gone With the Wind*.

TBS' list of firsts is long. CNN began transmission to the People's Republic of China and initiated the production of Spanish-language broadcasts to Latin America; instigated, sponsored, and broadcast the Goodwill Games, an international sports competition; began CNN Airport Network, a news service that delivers live broadcasting to air travelers; started the Cartoon Network and Turner Classic Movies network; continued to acquire film and television production companies to bring film libraries as well as production capabilities into its fold; branched into educational programming to the nation's schools; launched CNNfn, the financial network; partnered with *Sports Illustrated* to bring viewers CNN/Sports Illustrated, a 24-hour sports news network, which went on the air with 4.5 million subscribers; added the Better Health Network for viewing in medical offices; and launched the first 24-hour Spanish-language network, CNN en Español.

TBS' reach is worldwide. Its entertainment networks are among the most watched in the United States, and nearly 78 million people subscribe to CNN. Across the globe, more than 1 billion people have access to some CNN service.

THE MERGER

Nineteen ninety-six was a watershed year for Turner Broadcasting. Media giant Time Warner merged with TBS, and Turner was named vice chairman. Although Turner has a little more time to devote to various philanthropic efforts, he is very much involved in the company, says McGuirk, and continues to oversee all of TBS and its entities, including the three sports teams, as well as HBO (Home Box Office) and New Line Cinema, an independent producer and distributor of motion pictures.

TBS' go-get-'em culture has not been subdued by the merger, and, according to McGuirk, "TBS is as committed as ever to long-term growth in our home community of Atlanta and around the world. Turner Broadcasting System, Inc. will be around for a very long time to come. We will continue to adapt to the ever changing cable industry and world. Atlanta is home to us; the company's headquarters has always been here, and will remain here."

YKK Corporation of America

WHAT DO ZIPPERS HAVE TO DO WITH ATLANTA'S GEORGIA DOME? SURprisingly, there is a close and important connection. As the home football team, the Falcons, and their opponents charge, block, and tackle on the Dome's artificial turf, little does anyone realize that it's actually fastened together by yards and yards of YKK zippers. Not only that, but the glass in the Dome's windows and entrances is held in place by aluminum glazing systems produced by the architectural products company of YKK, YKK AP America Inc.

LITTLE PARTS. BIG DIFFERENCE.

Having come to this country in 1960, and to Georgia and its Atlanta headquarters in 1970, YKK (U.S.A.) Inc. currently holds the lion's share of the U.S. zipper market. It produces in Macon more than 1,500 styles of metal and plastic zippers. Amazingly, quantities approach some 7 million every day. In addition to fastening football fields, various YKK zippers also weather intense heat and drenchings in firemen's jackets, keep luggage safely closed despite rough handling, withstand daily abuse in school jackets and kids' jeans, proclaim a fashion statement in designer apparel, secure oil spill booms and fish farm nets, and much more. Since these hardy closures are often a product's only moving component, performance is critical. As the company's slogan says, "YKK. Little Parts. Big Difference."

With headquarters also in Atlanta, sister company YKK AP began in 1984 and has grown to become a recognized leader in the construction industry. It too has its manufacturing home in Georgia. Located in Dublin off I-16, the 500,000-square-foot state-of-the-art manufacturing plant had its start-up in 1992. Today it produces and finishes aluminum extrusions, and fabricates architectural building products of unsurpassed quality. These innovative systems are used in low, middle, and high-rise commercial buildings, many of which have become landmarks. Atlanta's Coca-Cola World Pavilion and Turner Field are but two.

CLOCKWISE FROM TOP:
THE GEORGIA DOME FEATURES CURTAIN-WALL AND ENTRANCE SYSTEMS BY YKK AP, A YKK CORPORATION OF AMERICA COMPANY.

ATLANTA'S TURNER FIELD USES HIGH-QUALITY STOREFRONT AND ENTRANCE SYSTEMS BY YKK AP.

YKK ZIPPERS, PLUS COLOR-COORDINATED HOOK AND LOOP, ADD STYLE AND DURABILITY TO THIS JACKET.

WITH THE USE OF COMPUTER-AIDED DESIGN, YKK FIELD TECH ENGINEERS CAN PRODUCE MACHINES AND MACHINE PARTS IN-HOUSE.

COMPOA/RALPH BRYAN

The parent company of YKK USA and YKK AP is YKK Corporation of America which has headquarters in Atlanta and offices in Macon and in Lyndhurst, New Jersey. These three firms help comprise a 14-company YKK America Group which employs more than 3,500 people across five time zones—including Canada, the United States, Mexico, Central America, the Caribbean, and South America. More than 1,500 of these employees live and work in Georgia.

Additional products manufactured by companies within the YKK America Group include specialty hook and loop fasteners, plastic and metal notions, buckles, snaps, buttons, rivets and burrs, hooks and eyes, and webbings used in a broad range of medical, sports, fashion, automotive, marine, and heavy industrial applications.

The Cycle of Goodness

YKK America Group is part of the vast YKK Corporation. Founded in 1934 and head-quartered in Japan, it is still privately held. Currently, the firm has in its network more than 80 subsidiaries in more than 50 countries around the world.

The companies of YKK America Group share a unique philosophy and a resulting way of doing business. As a teenager, the late Tadao Yoshida, YKK founder, was profoundly influenced by the autobiography of Andrew Carnegie, the Scottish-born American industrialist and philanthropist. Carnegie's book propounded the importance of one's obligation to society and provided the inspiration for Mr. Yoshida's philosophy. Called the Cycle of Goodness, it states simply, "No one prospers unless he renders benefit to others."

One way Mr. Yoshida practiced this concept was by manufacturing only useful, high-quality zippers that would enhance the products in which they were used. Since YKK zippers were the primary functioning parts, he believed they must perform perfectly over a long period of time so that the end-use merchandise would last longer and perform better. When it did, more articles would be sold to consumers who would enjoy increased value. As customers prospered, the demand for YKK products would also increase. With shared prosperity, the community would benefit, and all would prosper.

In a very real way, the Cycle of Goodness was responsible for YKK's coming to Georgia. The principle demands that wherever YKK goes to sell a product, for the good of the local community, YKK manufactures there. Thus, by 1972, YKK USA was ready to begin zipper manufacturing within the United States. Mr. Yoshida and a site selection team had narrowed their focus to the Southeast because by then, most of YKK's customer base was manufacturing there.

A key ingredient to YKK's decision to select Georgia was the state's then Governor Jimmy Carter who met Yoshida during this time. They formed an abiding mutual respect and became lifelong personal friends. It was Carter who helped convince Yoshida that Georgia was the place to be. But Georgia had a lot going for it on its own—particularly in the Macon area, which was near a deepwater port, interstate highways, the city of Atlanta, and a major airport, and was home to an eager and enthusiastic potential workforce.

The Cycle of Goodness remains the foundation of YKK. From architectural products to zippers, it pervades every facet of the company's organization, "not only in relations with our employees, customers, and the communities in which we are citizens, but also in our overall approach to business," notes Jay Takahashi, president of YKK Corporation of America.

A case in point is the company's total Vertically Integrated Production System. Throughout its manufacturing operations, YKK produces almost every component that goes into its products.

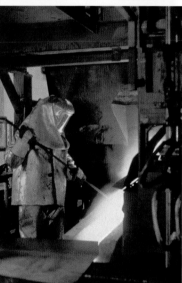

"One of our business principles is to get as close as possible to perfection," explains Takahashi, "and the best way to do that is to produce whatever we can ourselves—from raw materials to finished product. For example, in Macon, we have our own foundry where we produce brass that is exactly right in formula and shape for fasteners. In Dublin, we anodize extrusions through a vertical immersion process to create a lasting finish unmatched in the industry. Vertically integrated production is the best method of controlling quality, delivery, and cost at every step. This method ensures product availability and the consistency our customers have come to expect."

YKK has grown dramatically since its inception and will continue to grow in the new millennium. "Our focus is on the global picture. We partner innovatively with customers, and we're where they need us to be," Takahashi says. "As part of a strong and dynamic worldwide network, YKK can and does invest heavily in R&D to advance the industry and our products. We also provide field tech services to give our customers a strategic competitive edge. Now, we must become even more flexible, improve information exchange with customers, and grow together with them as we meet the challenges of the future."

WEBBINGS, PLASTIC BUCKLES AND NOTIONS, HOOK AND LOOP FASTENING TAPES, AND METAL FASTENERS ARE ALL QUALITY PRODUCTS PRODUCED BY YKK AMERICA GROUP COMPANIES (TOP).

AT THE YKK USA BRASS-WIRE PLANT IN MACON, BRASS IS PRODUCED TO FORM BASIC ZIPPER PARTS—ZIPPER TEETH, SLIDERS, AND TOP AND BOTTOM STOPS—PLUS FASTENERS FOR OTHER YKK AMERICA GROUP COMPANIES (BOTTOM).

Metropolitan Atlanta Rapid Transit Authority (MARTA)

METROPOLITAN ATLANTA RAPID TRANSIT AUTHORITY (MARTA), THE METRO Atlanta area's bus and rapid rail system, made history in 1996 as the first transit system to be designated the Official Provider of Public Transportation for the Olympic Games. During the 1996 Centennial Summer Olympic Games, MARTA carried more than 1.5 million daily passengers to venues throughout the Olympic city. People from

METROPOLITAN ATLANTA RAPID TRANSIT AUTHORITY (MARTA), THE REGIONAL BUS AND RAPID RAIL SYSTEM, HAS ONE OF THE LARGEST FLEETS OF CLEAN-FUEL, COMPRESSED-NATURAL-GAS BUSES IN THE COUNTRY.

DURING THE 1996 CENTENNIAL SUMMER OLYMPIC GAMES, MARTA CARRIED MORE THAN 1.5 MILLION DAILY PASSENGERS TO VENUES THROUGHOUT THE OLYMPIC CITY, INCLUDING THE GEORGIA TECH AQUATICS CENTER.

around the world were joyfully packed elbow-to-elbow on the trains, where they engaged in conversations, exchanged opinions and information, and traded commemorative pins while enjoying MARTA's contribution to their Olympic experience.

MARTA prepared years ahead for that summer event. The completion of new rail line extensions was met with unprecedented cooperation from city, state, and federal agencies, as well as corporations and nonprofit organizations. One of the most lasting effects to MARTA of the Olympic Games was the increase in ridership. Tens of thousands of metro Atlantans discovered that mass transit was safe, reliable, convenient, and affordable. MARTA spread the word with "Take MARTA. It's Smarta!," expressing the many benefits of its bus and rail services. Consequently, the Authority achieved a 9 percent increase in ridership over a two-year period after the Olympic Games.

Today, MARTA's sleek trains and colorful buses carry nearly

74.5 million passengers every year. With 240 railcars, 36 rail stations, and more than 700 buses serving 154 routes, MARTA is the seventh-largest transit system in the country, traveling a total of 52 million miles each year. By the end of 2000, the Authority will have one of the largest fleets of clean-fuel, compressed natural gas buses in the country.

FIRST THERE WERE MULES

Public transportation has been operating in Atlanta since 1871. The first transit system was a two-mile-long track for horse- and mule-drawn streetcars. As the city grew, so did its public transportation. By 1894, electricity-powered streetcars had replaced mule power. At the turn of the century, buses appeared on the scene, and then came electric streetcars that ran on tires with overhead wires. In 1963, the last of these were retired, and gasoline-powered buses took over the streets of Atlanta.

The first serious suggestions for a rapid transit system in the city were presented in a regional planning guide in 1952. Years later, the suggestions became more definite and the need more imminent. By 1960, a proposal had been made for a distinct rapid transit system. Within the same time, Atlanta found itself caught up in a period of explosive growth. With a booming economy and a new skyline under construction, thousands of newcomers and their automobiles arrived to add their energy to the city and congestion to the roads. The city continued to sprawl outward, and the need for a rapid transit system in the metro area was painfully obvious.

MARTA Takes Shape

Armed with studies, reports, and plans, a growing number of transit proponents pushed to bring rapid transit to Atlanta through public education committees, discussions, and lobbying at the local and state levels. As a result, the Georgia General Assembly passed the Metropolitan Atlanta Rapid Transit Authority Act in March 1965, and in January of the following year, the agency was created. In November 1971, a special rapid transit referendum was passed in two major metro counties (Fulton and DeKalb), adding a 1 percent sales tax to partially fund MARTA services.

When MARTA purchased the Atlanta Transit System, the metro area's existing bus service, a number of improvements were introduced over the next several years. The Authority received substantial funding from the federal Urban Mass Transportation Administration to begin construction and design of Atlanta's rapid rail system and make improvements to its bus routes. The biggest news came when MARTA broke ground for its rail line in 1975. Four years later, citizens crowded onto the trains for MARTA's inaugural trip on the East Line.

Growing with Atlanta

Today, rail lines and buses run in all directions across metro Atlanta. Beyond Atlanta, MARTA is looking toward the future to its role in a regional

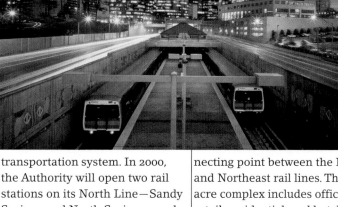

transportation system. In 2000, the Authority will open two rail stations on its North Line—Sandy Springs and North Springs—and will add 100 new railcars to keep pace with the increasing ridership demand of metro Atlanta. Future plans include expansion through Fulton and DeKalb counties to the east, south, north, and west.

As Atlanta continues to grow, issues of traffic, congestion, and air quality must be addressed. One solution MARTA has embraced involves land use policies and specifically the introduction of transit-oriented development. This concept of creating a dense mixed-use environment is one that will certainly support the quality of life that has attracted so many people to Atlanta. MARTA has always believed in a vision of transit-oriented development around its stations. Fulfilling its vision, MARTA has developed the immediate area surrounding the Lindbergh Center Station, a con-

necting point between the North and Northeast rail lines. The 47-acre complex includes office, retail, residential, and hotel opportunities for a "live, work, play" concept. Major developers, builders, and employers have pledged their faith and dollars in transit-oriented development. Nearly every MARTA station has the capacity for transit-oriented development, and the future looks bright for both MARTA and the metropolitan area.

The presence of public transportation has always signified growth and cosmopolitan progress. Since its inception, MARTA has been instrumental in establishing Atlanta as a world-class city. As metro Atlanta continues to grow by leaps and bounds, the role of transportation becomes ever more prevalent. This is not only a testament of mass transit, but also a prelude to a new and bright future for metropolitan Atlanta.

Westin Peachtree Plaza Hotel

THE WESTIN PEACHTREE PLAZA HOTEL IS A LANDMARK OF MODERN Atlanta. The tall, cylindrical tower rose in 1976, situated among new buildings that marked the beginning of a phenomenal cycle of growth and a brand-new skyline for the city. Located on a high point along Peachtree Street—originally a Cherokee and Creek Indian trail that followed a ridge in the Appalachian Piedmont—and 73 stories high,

the building to this day maintains its claim as the tallest hotel in North America and the Western Hemisphere.

REVOLUTIONARY DESIGN

John Portman, whose firm, John Portman & Associates, designed the Peachtree Plaza Hotel, is the father of the soaring hotel atrium. He revolutionized design in the hotel industry, beginning with his Atlanta projects and reaching to cities throughout the world. "The name and the architecture of the Westin Peachtree Plaza Hotel are known around the globe," says hotel General Manager Kerry Ringham, "and we attract a large number of interna-

tional visitors for both leisure and business travel."

The hotel's location, connected to the Atlanta Market Center, just steps from Atlanta's rapid rail system and within walking distance of all downtown convention sites and major-league sports facilities, gives the hotel a dominant role in the city's thriving tourist and convention business. Its own fully equipped meeting space, exhibit hall, and ballrooms draw groups year-round.

The Westin Peachtree Plaza offers its guests a variety of amenities, among them a fitness center, a sun deck, a swimming pool, concierge service, and a business center with full services for

business travelers. But the hotel also welcomes an unusually high number of local and regional guests. "An element in the uniqueness of this hotel is that we are a place for memories," notes Ringham. "We know in tracing our history of guests that we are a destination hotel. We are much more than a convenient place to stay; people come to Atlanta and plan especially to stay in this hotel."

Most of the facility's 1,068 rooms, including its six luxury suites, are rooms with a view, enhanced by floor-to-ceiling windows. Its entrance level provides access to the shopping gallery and several restaurants and cafés. The dramatic lobby, with its five-story atrium, is styled after Copenhagen's Tivoli Gardens. Marble flooring and sparkling lights combined with intimate seating areas and one-of-a-kind sculptures create a memorable atmosphere for visitors, whether they are local residents from nearby towns and suburbs; travelers from North Carolina, New York, or California; or guests from Tokyo, London, or Caracas.

The site of the hotel is in itself historic. It was the location of Atlanta's Governor's Mansion (originally the home of banker John James) from 1870 to 1921. That building was razed to make way for the Henry Grady Hotel, a premier hotel that hosted guests for decades.

ATLANTA IN VIEW

The Westin Peachtree Plaza's pièce de résistance is the Sun Dial revolving restaurant and bar, soaring 723 feet above Atlanta with panoramic views of the city and its environs. The Sun Dial is reached by

THE WESTIN PEACHTREE PLAZA HOTEL'S PIÈCE DE RÉSISTANCE IS THE SUN DIAL REVOLVING RESTAURANT AND BAR, SOARING 723 FEET ABOVE ATLANTA WITH PANORAMIC VIEWS OF THE CITY AND DISTANT FEATURES LIKE KENNESAW MOUNTAIN, STONE MOUNTAIN, HARTSFIELD AIRPORT 12 MILES TO THE SOUTH, MIDTOWN, AND POINTS BEYOND.

vation, attributes upon which the company has built its business.

Siemens holds more than 6,600 patents from its U.S. operations and more than 41,000 worldwide. Each company in the Siemens family can benefit from the break-throughs of its sister companies in an exchange of best-in-class methods. "Throughout its history, Siemens has been one of the world's most research-intensive companies," says Malott.

One example of the benefits of exchange in research is SE&A's development of manufacturing equipment that can handle components smaller than a grain of rice. At Motorola, SE&A's SIPLACE® surface mount assembly machines anchor the high-speed manufacturing lines used in the production of cable modems—devices that bring instant Internet and Web access to the rapidly growing number of users at home and in the workplace. SIPLACE technology makes it possible to assemble the diverse components of each modem's complex internal hardware with greater speed and accuracy in a smaller, more economical package.

PROVIDING TOTAL SOLUTIONS

Siemens Energy & Automation is comprised of four divisions: Distribution Products, Industrial Products, Industrial Systems & Technical Services, and Sales. The Distribution Products division focuses on products that control and distribute the flow of electricity for the industrial, commercial, and residential construction markets. Among its products are lighting control panels, switchboards, disconnect switches, and the familiar residential circuit breakers. These items make it possible for power users—whether a consumer or a huge manufacturing operation—to have electricity in the necessary amount when and where it is needed.

The Industrial Products division manufactures motors and drives in a spectrum of sizes; pumps and compressors; industrial controls, such as motor starters and overload relays; and industrial automation products and systems. SE&A's customers for these products are original equipment manufacturers (OEMs), specialty control markets, dis-

tributors, industrial manufacturing facilities, and utilities.

The Industrial Systems & Technical Services division integrates a vast array of the company's industrial products, as well as those from other manufacturers, to deliver best-system solutions to customers. This division designs, engineers, and markets turnkey projects for industrial customers, particularly those in the metals, paper, mining, and process industries.

Through a nationwide network of locally based service personnel, Siemens Westinghouse Technical Services offers solutions ranging from general contracting, installation, and start-up to plant modernization, maintenance, and equipment management programs, as well as information technology services, to industrial customers.

Over the years, the company has grown through expansion of markets and through acquisition, bringing into its group some of the most respected names in systems, technology, and technical services. The list includes Texas Instruments, Furnas Electric, Crouse-Hinds, and Westinghouse. "Each addition has contributed to the broadening of our products, systems, and services," says Malott. "We will continue to add strategic acquisitions that enhance our ability to provide a total solution to our customers."

RARE Hospitality International, Inc.

IN 1982, A RARE SNOWSTORM SHUT DOWN THE CITY OF ATLANTA AND SAVED a struggling little restaurant called LongHorn Steakhouse. It was early March when thick snow fell from the skies, forming layers on lawns, rooftops, and roadways. Virtually every company in the city sent its workers home early. With both cars and snow pouring onto the highways, massive gridlock ensued. Interstates and major arteries became parking lots of stranded vehicles and motorists.

On fabled Peachtree Street, George McKerrow Jr., founder and chairman of LongHorn Steaks, Inc.—now part of RARE Hospitality International, Inc.—ventured from his nearly empty restaurant into the storm and put up a sign that read, "Drinks $1.00 While It Snows." As commuters abandoned their cars and journeyed on foot to get home, LongHorn began to fill up. "That afternoon and evening we rang up $700 in the bar at $1 a drink," says McKerrow. LongHorn stayed open 24 hours a day for three days, feeding travelers trying to get home, as well as neighborhood residents who had lost electrical power.

COWBOY CUISINE

After months of barely scraping by since its August 1981 opening, the snowstorm marked the beginning of the restaurant's success. "That snowstorm introduced LongHorn to the neighborhood," says McKerrow. Nearly 20 years and more than 100 LongHorn Steakhouse restaurants later, the neighborhood and many other diners continue to patronize the Peachtree Long-Horn, as well as many others in 14 states throughout the Southeast and Midwest. Today, RARE Hospitality employs more than 12,000 people, and it served approximately 25 million meals in 1999.

The success of LongHorn Steakhouse proved McKerrow's belief that Atlanta was ready for what he calls cowboy cuisine—a Texas-style steakhouse that offers fun, casual dining with quality food in a colorful, spirited atmosphere. At the time, the concept was new not only to Atlanta, but also to cities and towns around the country. McKerrow's concept created the casual dining steakhouse niche. He is considered by many in the hospitality business to be the pioneer of casual steakhouse cuisine in America.

AN AMERICAN DREAM

Bitten by the restaurant and hospitality service bug at age 16, McKerrow went to work at Uncle John's Pancake House in Cleveland, Ohio. Only a year out of college, with a degree in political science and aspirations towards law, McKerrow set out on his entrepreneurial path when he bought and then sold a restaurant in West Virginia. He subsequently joined a national restaurant chain that brought him to Atlanta, where McKerrow was southeastern regional manager before leaving the company in 1980.

With the founding, survival, and growth of the LongHorn restaurants and RARE Hospitality,

IN 1982, A RARE SNOWSTORM IN EARLY MARCH SHUT DOWN THE CITY OF ATLANTA AND SAVED THE FIRST LONGHORN STEAKHOUSE. IN ORDER TO HELP STRANDED MOTORISTS, MCKERROW VENTURED FROM HIS NEARLY EMPTY RESTAURANT INTO THE STORM AND PUT UP A SIGN THAT READ, "DRINKS $1.00 WHILE IT SNOWS."

McKerrow says, "It is the American dream come true." He struggled through a rocky beginning, and even declared bankruptcy when his original partners pulled out of the venture before the first restaurant opened. The company was saved by new investors, including his father, George McKerrow Sr. "He stuck by me, even though I was a 30-year-old maverick and he was a corporate guy," says McKerrow.

Later, George McKerrow Sr. joined the company, and to this day, he remains active, particularly in corporate giving and RARE Hospitality's comprehensive charitable efforts. "He is the soul and spirituality of the company," says the younger McKerrow. "I count myself blessed that I have the opportunity to work with my father and know him in a way I could never have otherwise."

George McKerrow Jr. believes that RARE Hospitality—which also includes two other steak-house concepts, Bugaboo Creek Steakhouse and The Capital Grille—has attracted people who really care about service and customers, from corporate staff to restaurant managers and servers. President and CEO Phil Hickey Jr. is one of those people. With an extensive restaurant background, he came on board after RARE stumbled in 1996 and 1997.

THE LONGHORN ATTITUDE

After taking the company public in 1992 and guiding its success, McKerrow tried retirement. But, he readily admits, the management team put in charge at that time lost sight of the principles on which the company was built. "For awhile, we became something we didn't want to be, and it cost us dearly in both customers and employees," McKerrow says. In 1997, he came out of retirement and took the reins again. "We had to reinstall the LongHorn attitude," says McKerrow. As a result, he persuaded Hickey to join RARE as president and CEO.

"True service means the organization lives to serve those people who work for it," says Hickey. In doing so, a strong, stable, and loyal workforce is created that, in turn, creates stable and loyal customers. It becomes a self-perpetuating cycle. "Understanding that cycle is critical to good business performance," says Hickey.

In the intensely competitive restaurant business, it is excellent service that differentiates one company from the next in the marketplace. Says McKerrow, "As we grow nationally, we have the capability to change lives by providing a positive experience for both our employees and our guests, as RARE goes into the 21st century."

The Carter Center

WAGING PEACE, FIGHTING DISEASE, AND BUILDING HOPE: IN THE UNITED States and in countries across the globe, The Carter Center reaches out to leaders at the highest levels of government and to villagers in the poorest areas of the world to carry out its mission. Established by former President Jimmy Carter and his wife, Rosalynn, in 1982 in partnership with Emory University, the center manifests the couple's belief that service to humankind can reduce suffering and improve the quality of life for people worldwide.

WORKING TOGETHER

The nonpartisan and nonpolitical institute was formed just one year after the end of Carter's 1977-1981 term as president. "We searched our hearts for ways to use our unique position to help those less fortunate here in America and around the world. Always mindful of the power of faith to unite people, we undertook our own act of faith and founded The Carter Center," says Carter.

The Carter Center has brought together diverse people and groups to work toward common goals in peace and health with exceptional results. "It's a lesson," says Carter, "that no matter what our beliefs and political experiences, for the most part, we all want the same thing for our children and ourselves."

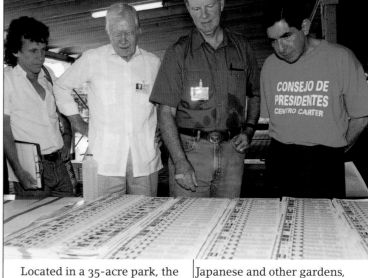

Located in a 35-acre park, the center overlooks Atlanta's skyline. The Carter Presidential Center complex includes the nonprofit Carter Center and the Jimmy Carter Library and Museum, owned and operated by the National Archives and Records Administration of the federal government. Also in the complex are a nondenominational chapel, Japanese and other gardens, natural wooded areas, ponds, and a meadow.

TEACHING PEOPLE

On the center's grounds, a life-size bronze sculpture depicts a common African village scene—a young boy leading his elder, whose sight has been damaged or stolen by river blindness,

A PROUD SASAKAWA-GLOBAL 2000 (SG 2000) FARMER SHARES HER EXPERIENCES WITH CARTER. SG 2000 WAS ESTABLISHED JOINTLY BY THE CARTER CENTER AND THE SASAKAWA AFRICA ASSOCIATION TO HELP FARMERS THROUGHOUT AFRICA INCREASE AGRICULTURAL PRODUCTION.

by the end of a stick. Since 1996, the center has worked through a global coalition to provide more than 12 million treatments with the drug Mectizan® in Latin America and parts of Africa to people afflicted by this parasitic eye disease. With poor health a major deterrent to economic growth, the center also spearheads efforts to control other diseases, and is responsible for leading a coalition that soon will make the water-borne Guinea worm disease only the second, after smallpox, to be eradicated worldwide. "We do not go into a country to foster dependency or to create a new bureaucracy. We go to educate people and to provide resources so they can improve their own lives," says Carrie Harmon, center spokesperson.

The Carter Center is fighting additional diseases and also promoting agriculture, particularly in Africa, to help farmers improve methods and crop yields. Suffering from widespread famine in the mid-1980s, Ethiopia now not only produces record crops, but in 1997 exported maize to Kenya. It was a success beyond the greatest hopes of Ethiopia's leaders and people.

The center also promotes peace in troubled areas around the world. Known for brokering for the his-

toric Camp David peace accords in 1978, the former president and his wife have provided vision and leadership in recent years for the center's work in China, Nicaragua, Venezuela, Sudan, Haiti, Liberia, Nigeria, and other countries where people thirst for peace and democracy. The center monitors and

mediates multiparty elections in emerging democracies, seeks peaceful solutions to civil conflict, promotes economic cooperation among nations, and works to strengthen respect for human rights and the role of a free press worldwide. The Carter Center is faith in action.

IN APRIL 1993, CARTER JOINED MORE THAN 7,000 VOLUNTEERS IN A DOOR-TO-DOOR DRIVE SPONSORED BY THE CARTER CENTER TO IDENTIFY CHILDREN IN ATLANTA WHO NEEDED IMMUNIZATIONS. NEARLY 16,000 PRESCHOOL CHILDREN EITHER RECEIVED FREE SHOTS OR HAD THEIR VACCINATION RECORDS UPDATED.

Georgia-Pacific Corporation

GEORGIA-PACIFIC CORPORATION'S (G-P) PRODUCTS ARE USED AROUND THE world. They are found inside and outside commercial buildings and homes—from roof decking to wooden subfloors, and from reams of communication paper and cardboard boxes to paper towels in the kitchen. One of the world's largest forest products companies, G-P manufactures and distributes building products and pulp

and paper products through its Georgia-Pacific Group. In addition, through its operating entity The Timber Company, it manages about 4.8 million acres of forestland in the United States.

Headquartered in Atlanta since 1982, the company began as a modest lumber wholesale venture in Augusta, Georgia, in 1927. A young salesman named Owen R. Cheatham borrowed $6,000, added another $6,000 of his own money, and launched his business as Georgia Hardwood Lumber Co. Within a few years, the company began manufacturing operations as well. As ambitious as Cheatham

surely was, he could hardly have imagined the current global scope and vast operations of the company he founded.

Georgia Hardwood first went public in 1949, and after making several acquisitions in the Northwest, added Pacific to its name. Georgia-Pacific moved its headquarters from Georgia to Olympia in 1953, and a year later, to Portland, Oregon. Now in its eighth decade, Georgia-Pacific Corporation has combined annual revenues that exceed $18 billion, and it is one of the 10 largest public companies in Georgia. The company employs some 55,000 people, and has more than 500 plants, mills, distribution centers, and offices.

GROWTH THROUGH EXPANSION AND ACQUISITIONS

Through expansion and acquisitions, Georgia-Pacific has grown to become a world leader in its industry. The company has made major acquisitions that have taken it beyond lumber sales and milling into the pulp and paper business, corrugated containers, tissue, chemicals, plywood, gypsum (a mineral used to make plaster) products, and timberland. One of G-P's largest recent expansions was its merger with Great Northern Nekoosa Corporation in 1990—a move that added 58 plants and mills, 83 paper distribution centers, and nearly $3 billion in revenues. "We have sought acquisitions that we believe fit our strategy for growth and product expansion," says Chairman and CEO A.D. "Pete" Correll. "We expect to continue to identify other candidates and add those that make a good fit."

In 1997, G-P split its operations into two segments: Georgia-Pacific Group and The Timber Company. Georgia-Pacific Group comprises

several manufacturing and distribution businesses for building products, pulp, and paper, while The Timber Company is in the business of growing and selling timber and wood fiber. The Timber Company—which is the third-largest private owner of timberland in this country—manages timberland and sells various softwoods, hardwoods, and pulpwoods to the Georgia-Pacific Group and industrial wood users. It sells about 60 percent of its timber to its sister company. "These are two distinct businesses, and this separation allows each business to be totally responsible for its own performance and financial and strategic flexibility," says Correll.

In June 1999, G-P made a $1.5 billion bid for the nation's largest distributor of paper products and janitorial supplies: Pennsylvania-based Unisource Worldwide Inc. The deal would bring paper distribution in-house, since Unisource already distributes Georgia-Pacific paper products. It is, according to Correll, "a logical move" to support the company's paper business.

COMMUNITY COMMITMENT

As G-P expanded nationwide, with extensive operations in the Southeast, the company moved back home to Georgia in 1982. In doing so, Georgia-Pacific made a serious commitment to Atlanta with the construction of its monolithic pink granite headquarters building on Peachtree Street in the heart of the city. Dramatic sculptures by internationally renowned sculptor Louise Nevelson grace the lobby and other public spaces, and the company sponsored the construction of a branch of Atlanta's High Museum of Art in the building. The branch, the High Museum of Folk Art and Photography Galleries, continues to present works of local, national, and international artists in these fields.

In the past, Georgia-Pacific's leaders have demonstrated their commitment to the Atlanta community, and the company's present CEO, Correll, is no exception. He is a visible, active advocate of the city, and works energetically in matters of education and Atlanta's growth and quality of life. Through the Georgia-Pacific Foundation, the company supports a number of community programs, not only in

its home city, but also in the hundreds of communities in which the company has operations.

CONSIDERING THE ENVIRONMENT

Georgia-Pacific has joined the growing number of companies that recognize the impact of industry on the environment. In 1994, the company adopted its environmental and safety principles. Among the issues addressed are management's commitment, employee training and education, and auditing and performance programs that provide feedback on how effectively the company is putting its principles into practice. Also among the principles are pollution prevention, sustainable development and forest management, conservation of natural resources, energy efficiency, employee safety and health, waste reduction, technological innovation, response to community concerns, and voluntary disclosure of the company's performance and progress against its set goals.

It's an ambitious effort, but one that Georgia-Pacific has continued to address, despite challenges. "Since we began this program, environmental protection and safety have moved beyond being special programs and have become a way of life and business at the company," says Correll. The list of accomplishments and improvements, from participation in international environmental programs and entire G-P plants and mills to individual contributions, proves the effectiveness of such a company-backed effort.

ONE OF THE WORLD'S LARGEST FOREST PRODUCTS COMPANIES, GEORGIA-PACIFIC MANAGES ABOUT 4.8 MILLION ACRES OF FORESTLAND IN THE UNITED STATES THROUGH ITS OPERATING ENTITY THE TIMBER COMPANY.

GEORGIA-PACIFIC IS A MAJOR MANUFACTURER AND DISTRIBUTOR OF BUILDING MATERIALS, AS WELL AS PULP, PAPER, AND RELATED CHEMICALS USED IN PAPERMAKING.

BellSouth Corporation

**B**ellSouth Corporation—formerly a Baby Bell company—was formed upon the 1984 divestiture of AT&T. Since that time, few could have imagined the dramatic changes that lay ahead for the newly established company or the advances in technology that would drive those changes. ❑ Today, BellSouth has gone from being a local telephone services provider to a $25 billion communications services company providing telecommunications, wireless communications, cable and digital TV, directory advertising and publishing, and Internet and data services. The company has surpassed its original southeastern market to reach more than 33 million customers in nearly 20 countries.

New Horizons

Among the fastest-growing segments of BellSouth's business are wireless and data services. "Almost half of all traffic on the BellSouth telecommunications network is data, surpassing voice for the first time.

BELLSOUTH CORPORATION IS A $25 BILLION COMMUNICATIONS SERVICES COMPANY PROVIDING TELECOMMUNICATIONS, WIRELESS COMMUNICATIONS, CABLE AND DIGITAL TV, DIRECTORY ADVERTISING AND PUBLISHING, AND INTERNET AND DATA SERVICES.

Voice is not declining; in fact it continues to grow, doubling every 12 years. But, data traffic over the Internet—such as E-mail and retail orders—continues to double every 100 to 120 days," says Duane Ackerman, BellSouth CEO and chairman.

In addition, BellSouth's wireless services have fueled tremendous growth in the international arena, resulting in nearly 10 million wireless customers throughout the world. Although BellSouth provides wireless services in Denmark, Germany, New Zealand, Israel, and Asia, the company looks southward to Latin America for its most dramatic impact. BellSouth entered the Argentinean market in 1993, and today, the company is the dominant wireless provider in Latin America with more than 4 million customers.

The company continues to grow in other communications areas as well. Its Internet company, BellSouth.net, is one of the fastest-growing Internet service providers in the country. BellSouth Entertainment provides crystal-clear digital television service in Atlanta and key markets throughout the region. And BAPCO, the company's white and yellow pages directory company, which is also headquartered in Atlanta, is one of the world's largest directory companies, producing more than 1,000 directories every year. The company's strategy is to grow its customer base in current operations, evolve the cellular business to include a wider array of telecommunications services, and expand its Latin American market.

Commitment to Atlanta

Throughout BellSouth's history, the company has always been a visible leader in the communities it serves. Despite BellSouth's worldwide expansion, the company has looked closely at its headquarters city of Atlanta.

In January 1999, BellSouth made an announcement advocating a new commitment to the city and the quality of life in the metro area. The company plans to network three new business centers by locating them on Metropolitan Atlanta Rapid Transit Authority (MARTA), Atlanta's rapid rail system. The centers will be located inside the I-285 perimeter highway that circles Atlanta, and are scheduled to be completed in phases between 2001 and 2003. This plan will consolidate some 13,000 of the corporation's 19,000 Atlanta-based employees who are spread out among 75 locations in and around the city.

"Our plans for the Atlanta metro area are based on quality-of-life issues," says Ackerman. "This is an opportunity to take positive action in response to Atlanta's traffic congestion and environmental challenges. Public transportation is a powerful component in changing commuting habits."

BellSouth and its employees also take leadership roles in numerous other civic, charitable, and cultural activities in the Atlanta area. The company is typically the largest contributor to United Way's Atlanta campaign. It is a major supporter of the arts, such as the Woodruff Arts Center, and its executives have leadership roles in various Atlanta civic efforts such as the Chamber of Commerce, Central Atlanta Progress, and various education initiatives.

KETCHUM ATLANTA IS RECOGNIZED THROUGHOUT THE SOUTHEAST AS the region's largest full-service international public relations firm. "It's this agency's belief that the power of a good idea—creatively thought out and well executed—is unlimited," says Jane Shivers, partner and director of Ketchum. That fundamental belief characterizes Ketchum Atlanta's history and booming growth, and translates into an industry-leading reputation for client service and satisfaction.

GLOBAL REACH

It's a story that spans the globe, reaching from Ketchum's New York headquarters to more than 1,500 public relations professionals in 30 offices worldwide. The firm planted roots in Atlanta in 1985 with the acquisition of Shivers Communications, which Shivers formed in 1983. In 1996, Ketchum joined Omnicom, the world's largest communications holding company.

Ketchum Atlanta's growth parallels that of Atlanta's global business presence. "We're proud to have grown with our clients to serve their needs around the world," says Shivers. "Our passion for what we do keeps us motivated and dedicated."

For Ketchum Atlanta, that means delivering for clients like Delta Air Lines, Equifax, Southern Company, Orkin, Simmons Company, Bank of America, Bombardier Motor Corporation, Total Systems Services, IBM, Scientific-Atlanta, and Nokia.

Ketchum's Best Teams approach is a philosophy that promotes cross-network utilization of talent—extending Ketchum Atlanta's reach to account work around the world. This extended client family includes global powerhouses like FedEx, Visa, Wendy's International, Del Monte, Miller Brewing, Genentech, Bristol-Myers, and Pharmacia & Upjohn.

It's this global reach and depth of experience in Atlanta's dynamic communications marketplace that has created what even competitors describe as "one hot PR agency."

INDUSTRY-LEADING EXPERTISE

Ketchum's commitment to the power of good ideas and top client service shows through recognition for hard work and measurable results. The agency has won more Public Relations Society of America (PRSA) Silver Anvils—the most prestigious award in the industry—than any other PR firm in the business. Industry expertise has earned Ketchum multiple titles as *Inside PR*'s Agency of the Year.

Ketchum's global practices elevate client satisfaction by developing a deeper knowledge of their industries. Ketchum Atlanta offers specialty practice areas in brand marketing, corporate and workplace communications, creative services, and technology.

Ketchum's Atlanta office is also home to the company's Latin American and African-American marketing outreach—vital and expanding markets for Ketchum. In addition, a growing sports marketing effort has provided support for clients from the Final Four to the Super Bowl, and from NASCAR to speed boating.

Ketchum Creative Works, the agency's booming in-house graphic design center, also calls Atlanta home. The e-Ketchum interactive design group, which covers the scope of interactive media, including Internet, intranet, and a range of multimedia services, also radiates from Ketchum Atlanta.

BEST PEOPLE, BEST TEAMS, BEST SERVICE

It all goes back to Ketchum's core philosophy: best people, best teams, best service for clients. Known for its depth of talent, Ketchum's special practice fields are led by some of the most experienced and creative minds in the industry.

Ketchum's future will be defined by continued growth, innovation, motivation, and teamwork. "The world of marketing is far more complicated than ever," says Shivers. "Public relations is taking a leadership role in the marketing mix at home and internationally. We have many challenges ahead, but we have the excitement of knowing that we can really make a difference in the lives of our employees and our clients."

KETCHUM ATLANTA'S GROWING SPORTS MARKETING EFFORT HAS PROVIDED SUPPORT FOR MANY CLIENTS FROM THE FINAL FOUR TO THE SUPER BOWL, AND FROM NASCAR TO SPEED BOATING (TOP).

KETCHUM IS KNOWN THROUGHOUT THE INDUSTRY FOR ITS AWARD-WINNING PERFORMANCE, TAKING HOME MORE PUBLIC RELATIONS SOCIETY OF AMERICA (PRSA) SILVER ANVIL AWARDS THAN ANY OTHER FIRM IN THE BUSINESS AND EARNING MULTIPLE TITLES AS INSIDE PR'S AGENCY OF THE YEAR (BOTTOM).

1986

AMC GLOBAL COMMUNICATIONS, INC.

1986

COCA-COLA ENTERPRISES INC.

1987

JACKSON SECURITIES INCORPORATED

1988

BUCKHEAD COALITION, INC.

1990

WORLDSPAN®

1992

THE NORTH HIGHLAND COMPANY

1992

SHORTER COLLEGE

1993

WELLSTAR HEALTH SYSTEM

1994

INTERNET SECURITY SYSTEMS (ISS)

1996

MARIETTA CONFERENCE CENTER & RESORT

1997

THE LEADER PUBLISHING GROUP, INC.

1997

PLATINUM TELEVISION GROUP

1998

SHERATON ATLANTA HOTEL

© HAROLD DANIELS

AMC Global Communications, Inc.

IN TODAY'S WORLD, TELECOMMUNICATIONS IS FAST BECOMING THE KEYSTONE in a company's infrastructure and, as a result, telemanagement is essential in harnessing advanced communications capabilities. As a full-service telecommunications company, AMC Global Communications, Inc. is a leading provider of customized total communications solutions. AMC Global focuses on telecommunications hardware such as designing, implementing, and maintaining equipment for business and commercial customers whose needs range from four or five phones to hundreds of phones, and up to 60,000 ports for incoming lines, stations, and telephones.

With the skill, attention, and expertise of an artisan designing a complex mosaic, AMC Global brings together the pieces of telecommunications equipment and services—including long distance, voice mail, fax, automated attendant, external paging, call sequencers, patch panels, voice/data management, Internet access, and videoconferencing devices, among others—for its customers' specific business needs.

COMPETITIVE BUSINESS

With headquarters in metro Atlanta and offices in South Carolina and Florida, AMC Global primarily markets its services in the Southeast, while also serving a number of other businesses all over the country. The company has more than 11,000 customers, from locally owned companies and professional firms to Fortune 500 corporations.

Customers include manufacturers, distributors, auto dealers, banks, architects, builders, and attorneys.

To add to its selection of products and services, as well as to extend its geographic reach, AMC Global has formed strategic alliances with top companies such as NEC, Toshiba, Octel, BellSouth, Qwest, Key Voice Technologies, and Active Voice. As a result, AMC is one of the largest NEC and Toshiba dealers in the United States.

"Providing telecom services is a fiercely competitive business," says William Abram, AMC Global's founder, chairman, president, and CEO. Of the approximately 7,000 interconnect telephone companies in business today, AMC Global Communications is one of the largest in the nation and is listed among the top 30 in the Teleconnect 100 list.

GREAT EXPECTATIONS

Abram started his company in 1986 when he took on a client base of about 100 customers from a small company that had ceased operations. From the start, AMC Global was focused intently on customer service. Abram built a management team that believes AMC Global Communications is a service company whose business

MIKE SCHERER, VICE PRESIDENT-TECHNICAL SERVICES AT AMC GLOBAL COMMUNICATIONS, INC., LECTURES A CLASS ON TELECOMMUNICATIONS TECHNOLOGY (TOP).

WITH A FLEET OF VANS READY FOR DISPATCH, AMC GLOBAL IS ONE OF THE LEADING PROVIDERS OF TELECOMMUNICATION SERVICES IN ATLANTA AND THE UNITED STATES (BOTTOM).

is to serve its customers beyond their expectations. To this day, the original AMC team remains intact, including Jerry Inglima, executive vice president-sales and marketing; Michael Scherer, vice president-technical services; Joseph Thomas, operations manager; and Daniel Mollette, assistant vice president-sales and marketing.

AMC Global's first rule is to listen closely to customers to determine their unmet needs. Through this consultative approach, the company designs and implements technological telecommunications solutions unique to each customer. "We are in a highly charged, complex, constantly developing business," says Abram. "Our customers expect us to provide them with the systems to meet their unique telecommunications needs."

While AMC Global works closely with its customers, the company handles all phases of the installations, including such aspects as delivery of equipment and contacting the involved telecommunications carriers. It also handles switchover, training, and maintenance. This total turnkey approach is welcomed by customers with appreciation and relief, as is evident in the many letters of appreciation and thanks—often for service above and beyond expectations—that line the hallways of AMC Global's offices.

TRAINING IN TECHNOLOGY

One of AMC Global's greatest challenges is staying abreast of advancing technology. "There is an enormous amount of information out there," notes Abram. In order to provide the best solutions for customers, the company must understand and employ the most effective technology, which often means weeding through myriad new developments that enter the marketplace nearly every day. AMC Global's answer is to hire talented, committed people and to emphasize training. Manufacturers' training, technology seminars and conventions, and dealers' meetings all play a

part in the training for AMC's technical staff.

Additionally, the company provides trainers for its customers' service employees who operate the telecommunications systems. "Their comfort and productivity is critical," comments Abram. "It reflects on how well we have done our job, and it will help keep our customers satisfied with our products." This is an important factor since more than 65 percent of AMC Global's business is from repeat customers.

GIVING 110 PERCENT

AMC Global's customer-centered philosophy has grown into a corporate culture of giving 110 percent. Throughout its offices, employees such as the chairman, receptionist, technical wizards, sales manager, and mail clerk all wear small gold pins reading "110%." Says Abram, "I think everyone who works for AMC Global is proud of the company, its success, and the quality of work we do. Isn't that what everyone wants—to be proud of

where you work and what you do, and to share in that success?"

At AMC Global, the expectation that each employee will give 110 percent is a shared motive that creates a fellowship and sincere caring about the product the company delivers. Abram's strong commitment to the 110 percent principle and his motivational abilities have infused the company with this belief. Says Abram, "When you give 100 percent, you compete. When you give 110 percent, you succeed."

T. CLARK, DIRECTOR-ACCOUNT COORDINATION (SECOND FROM LEFT); WILLIAM ABRAM, PRESIDENT AND CEO; AND DANIEL MOLLETTE, ASSISTANT VICE PRESIDENT-SALES AND MARKETING (TOP)

WORKING CLOSELY WITH ITS CUSTOMERS, AMC GLOBAL OVERSEES ALL PHASES OF DELIVERY, INSTALLATION, AND MAINTENANCE OF EQUIPMENT, SUCH AS PBX TELEPHONE SYSTEMS (BOTTOM).

▶ MONICA NIKORE

▶ MONICA NIKORE

Jackson Securities Incorporated

WELL-MANAGED, PRODUCTIVE CAPITAL IS THE FOUNDATION FOR ANY STRONG corporation, institution, or government. Jackson Securities Incorporated is a full-service investment banking firm that has built a successful business providing sound investment banking solutions to help clients raise and manage capital efficiently and productively. Founded in Atlanta, the firm provides a full range of financial

services, including corporate, municipal, and structured finance; fixed-income and equity sales and trading; corporate financial advisory services; and Public Asset Leveraging®. The combination of client focus, experience, technical expertise, resources, and standards of excellence has been key to Jackson Securities' soaring reputation in investment banking. Leveraging their reputation for excellence in investment banking, the principals at Jackson Securities use the company's intellectual capital and financial technology to create a pipeline of reinvestment in the community.

STRONG LEADER, STRONG FOUNDATION

Few firms in investment banking have such a high-profile leader as Jackson Securities. The founder and chairman is Maynard H. Jackson, a former vice mayor and three-term successful mayor of Atlanta whose name is already in the history books. In 1974, he became the first African-American mayor of Atlanta. During his tenures (1974-1982 and 1990-1994), he installed modern management systems; reorganized government for greater efficiency; initiated the city's first neighborhood planning unit system and

first comprehensive development plan; organized business development offices in Asia and Europe; led the revitalization of 24 neighborhoods; established equal opportunity for minorities and women in city government employment and contracting; took leading stands on human rights issues; encouraged and structured the development of the arts for the masses of people; and was instrumental in Atlanta's successful effort to win the 1996 Centennial Olympic Games. Jackson led Atlanta's biggest brick-and-mortar administration that resulted in a new Hartsfield Atlanta International Airport, the building of a number of community service facilities, the opening of neighborhood arts centers, and dramatic improvements to the city's parks and infrastructure, including paving 123 miles of previously unpaved city streets.

Jackson applies that same leadership and energy to his investment banking and securities brokerage firm, Jackson Securities. Headquartered in downtown Atlanta, the company has offices in Houston, Dallas, Los Angeles, San Francisco, San Diego, Miami, and Orlando, with plans for others. Jackson Securities has participated in municipal bond underwriting transactions totaling tens of billions of dollars in more than 20 states. While participating in numerous municipal bond underwriting syndicates as senior manager, co-senior manager, or co-manager, Jackson Securities has received rave reviews for its performance, particularly as senior manager in transactions totaling hundreds of millions of dollars. With millions of dollars in assets and access

JACKSON SECURITIES INCORPORATED CHAIRMAN MAYNARD H. JACKSON (LEFT), EXECUTIVE VICE PRESIDENT AND CFO MILLICENT E. COUNTS, AND PRESIDENT AND CEO REUBEN R. MCDANIEL III HAVE IMPLEMENTED AGGRESSIVE STRATEGIES TO GROW THE COMPANY TO NATIONAL RECOGNITION AS INVESTMENT BANKING PROFESSIONALS WITH A MISSION OF COMMUNITY IMPROVEMENT.

through its banking relationships to tens of millions of dollars in additional risk capital, Jackson Securities is well capitalized to senior-manage municipal issues for cities, counties, states, school boards, and civil authorities.

A Complementary Pair for Expansion and Growth

Under the leadership of Chairman Jackson, a former bond lawyer, municipal finance became the core business for a rapidly expanding Jackson Securities. Jackson then named Reuben R. McDaniel III, president/CEO, to grow the company's participation in the capital markets. McDaniel has a strong reputation as an effective corporate manager who can analyze and structure the most complex financial deals and, at the same time, utilize his exceptional communication and

analytical skills to inform clients about the numbers in a way that is clear, concise, and understandable. He has assembled a team of investment bankers and institutional sales professionals who have earned reputations for excellence in understanding the capital markets and successfully applying their expertise to deliver cost-effective transactions for institutions, corporations, and public issuers of debt. "It was our shared commitment to integrity and quality, along with the opportunity to grow the firm, that drew me here," says McDaniel.

While the two men share a basic philosophy (and the same birthday), they complement each other in their skills and talents. Jackson focuses on strategic growth of the firm and business development, and McDaniel leads the effort to increase the firm's

senior-managed deals, expand the Sales and Trading Division, grow the client base in Structured Finance and Corporate Finance, and enhance the company's product diversity. While accomplishing these goals, it is the company's mission to utilize its intellectual capital and financial technology to deliver innovative solutions to its clients and, in the process, create opportunities for reinvestment in underserved communities.

Through financial structures in which Jackson Securities participates, the company can have a direct impact on these communities. "Whether we are structuring a financing for housing, community revitalization, economic and business development, school systems, water and sewer projects, transportation, or solid waste projects, we look for possibilities to enhance America's cities and to support minority communities," says McDaniel.

Together, Jackson, McDaniel, and Executive Vice President and CFO Millicent E. Counts have implemented aggressive strategies to grow Jackson Securities to national recognition as the leading company of investment banking professionals with a mission of community improvement.

In the area of product diversity, for example, Jackson Securities structures financial transactions to help companies with $50 million to $200 million in revenues gain access to capital. A key strength of Jackson Securities is its ability to structure innovative transactions in asset-backed mortgages, securitizations, collateralized mortgage obligations (CMOs), and other high-yield securities that offer its clients the returns they desire in fixed-income securities. "Our goal is to be the best investment banking firm, one that encompasses the diverse population that is America," comments Jackson. "We are a fully integrated firm, representing the ever increasing diversity of the workforce of today and the future. We—and all businesses—need skilled people of diverse backgrounds to find for our clients the most creative solutions to business challenges."

Public Entrepreneurism

Jackson's experience in public office has given him exceptional insights and an unusual perspective of the workings of local governments. It has led him to the concept of Public Asset Leveraging, which he maintains is a wave of the future. "Many governments do not know what they own," he says. "However, they should have a complete inventory of all assets, and they should identify the underperforming and nonperforming assets."

Since many governments are not well versed in business, local governments can turn to the private sector to manage the process of leveraging these public assets. Jackson includes this concept in a

term that he dubs public entrepreneurism. "One of our tasks is to educate the public and private sectors on the value of this concept," he adds.

Reaching Out and Giving Back

Jackson and McDaniel, as well as many members of Jackson Securities, have a history of reaching out to the communities they serve. In response to the devastating effects of poverty on children, Jackson established the Maynard Jackson Youth Foundation, Inc. (MJYF) in 1990 as a non-profit educational foundation. Its purpose is to provide positive leadership training, mentoring, and role-modeling programs for Atlanta's inner-city 11th graders. Jackson himself teaches most of the Leadership Academy classes, and graduates already have proved

themselves as standouts in universities and the armed forces. Recognizing the benefits that MJYF has provided them, many of its graduates give back by becoming peer trainers and role models for current students.

The programs are built on the premise that "the fight against poverty is best won by skilled leaders who have known poverty," says Jackson. "We are teaching young people to lead at a time in their lives when there is still hope for each of them. If we can provide leadership training that enhances character, then our goals will be realized. It is our dream that these young people will pursue the education and training that equip them for a successful life, and also provide them with an understanding of the money markets and their impact on this economy."

MAYNARD JACKSON YOUTH FOUNDATION PRESIDENT JOHN E. HOLLEY (STANDING, LEFT) AND FOUNDER, CHAIRMAN, AND PRINCIPAL TEACHER JACKSON TEACH BASIC LEADERSHIP, CRITICAL AND POSITIVE THINKING, SELF-ESTEEM, AND SALES SKILLS TO ATLANTA'S INNER-CITY 11TH GRADERS.

COCA-COLA ENTERPRISES INC. (CCE) MARKETS, PRODUCES, AND distributes liquid, nonalcoholic refreshment to customers and consumers in its franchise territories, which encompass some 353 million people throughout North America and western Europe. With more than 440 facilities and 66,000 employees, CCE is the world's largest bottler of liquid, nonalcoholic refreshment,

distributing some 3.8 billion (pro forma) unit cases of product in 1998.

Coca-Cola Enterprises sells approximately 74 percent of The Coca-Cola Company's bottle and can volume in North America and is the sole licensed bottler for products of The Coca-Cola Company in Belgium, Great Britain, France, Luxembourg, and the Netherlands. CCE also distributes Dr Pepper and several other beverage brands, as well as still and sparkling waters, juices, isotonics, and teas.

DEEP ROOTS

Coca-Cola Enterprises was formed 100 years after Coca-Cola syrup was first produced in 1886 by Atlanta pharmacist John Pemberton and sold at the neighborhood drugstore. CCE traces its business roots to 1899 when two Chattanooga entrepreneurs secured nationwide rights to bottle Coca-Cola. They set up a network of local franchises, a system that remained in place until the 1980s, when these bottling franchises began to consolidate.

In 1986, The Coca-Cola Company acquired two large bottling groups and combined them with some of its own bottling operations to create Coca-Cola Enterprises. It spun off the new company with a huge and successful initial stock offering in November that same year.

CCE experienced major growth in 1991, when it merged with the Johnston Coca-Cola Bottling Group, the original bottling franchise for Coca-Cola that was established in 1899. Summerfield K. Johnston Jr., the grandson of one of the founders of that company, took on the management of CCE until 1998, when he passed the torch to current President and CEO Henry A. Schimberg. Today, Johnston remains as chairman of the board.

EXPANDING A LOCAL BUSINESS

Schimberg attributes much of Coca-Cola Enterprises' success to employees. "This is truly a local business, and we have expanded our workforce with a diversity that reflects our broad consumer and customer base," says Schimberg. "We recognize that our most valuable and essential resource in our company is our people, and it is through our investment in the training and development of our employees that we ultimately grow the business."

CCE has taken its local operating philosophy to international locales. Venturing beyond U.S. borders first in 1993 to the Netherlands, the company now has operations in Belgium, Canada, France, Great Britain, and Luxembourg. More than 30 percent of CCE's volume is produced outside the United States.

With nearly two dozen acquisitions since 1996, Coca-Cola Enterprises has been the primary consolidator of bottling territories in North America and western Europe. "Our motivation is not to get bigger, but to get better. We embrace acquisition opportunities that we believe create value for the company and our share owners," says Schimberg. "Regardless of our size, we are and will remain a local Coca-Cola bottling company."

COCA-COLA ENTERPRISES INC. (CCE) MARKETS, PRODUCES, AND DISTRIBUTES LIQUID, NONALCOHOLIC REFRESHMENT TO CUSTOMERS AND CONSUMERS IN ITS FRANCHISE TERRITORIES, WHICH ENCOMPASS SOME 353 MILLION PEOPLE THROUGHOUT NORTH AMERICA AND WESTERN EUROPE (TOP).

CCE SELLS APPROXIMATELY 74 PERCENT OF THE COCA-COLA COMPANY'S BOTTLE AND CAN VOLUME IN NORTH AMERICA AND IS THE SOLE LICENSED BOTTLER FOR PRODUCTS OF THE COCA-COLA COMPANY IN BELGIUM, GREAT BRITAIN, FRANCE, LUXEMBOURG, AND THE NETHERLANDS (BOTTOM).

Buckhead Coalition, Inc.

BUCKHEAD COALITION, INC. HAS A CLEAR MISSION: THIS ORGANIZATION OF business and civic leaders works to nurture the quality of life in the Buckhead community and to help "coordinate orderly growth while balancing residential and commercial interests." It is a mission of major proportion in this affluent, fast-growing community. ❏ The Buckhead community had a very simple beginning.

Originally not much more than a tavern and store built by settler Henry Irby, this stop in the road took on the name Buckhead in 1838 when Irby mounted the head of a large buck on a post near the tavern. No one at that time could have realized what Buckhead would become.

THE BEVERLY HILLS OF THE EAST

A name today recognized throughout metro Atlanta, Buckhead is a distinctive community known for its beautiful homes, stately houses of worship, excellent schools, fine restaurants, upscale shopping, trendy nightspots, prestigious art galleries, luxury hotels, and high-rise office buildings. Often referred to as the Beverly Hills of the East, it is located within the boundaries of the City of Atlanta and encompasses approximately 28 square miles. More than 66,000 people live in Buckhead, and the area boasts the highest per capita income in the state. The heart of Buckhead's commercial district, which is the second-largest downtown in Georgia, is just four miles north of center-city Atlanta.

Few communities in the country have the advantage of high-powered advocates working together in a single organization. The Buckhead Coalition, founded in 1988, has a set number of 75 members (and a long waiting list) who are chief executives of major companies in Buckhead. They are established leaders who can make decisions quickly and who can raise money effectively. Members live and work in the area, and they have a vested interest in Buckhead's quality of life and its growth.

A MATTER OF BALANCE

Growth is a given in the foreseeable future, " says Buckhead Coalition President Sam Massell. "In fact, in 1994, Atlanta's city planners predicted that in Buckhead office space alone would triple in 15 years. We are in the midst of that building boom, as well as retail and residential expansion." A native Atlantan, as well as a businessman and a veteran of the Atlanta political arena, Massell served as a city councilman and was mayor of Atlanta from 1970 to 1974. He was tapped as president of the organi-

zation upon its formation by Buckhead businessman and civic leader, R. Charles Loudermilk Sr., chairman and CEO of Aaron Rents, Inc., a national furniture rental and sales company, whose headquarters is in Buckhead.

"What is critical is that the growth be balanced," says Massell. "The quality of life is what attracts people to Buckhead in the first place. We want to be very careful not to destroy the very thing that brings people and business here."

Achieving this balance is not easy, but the Buckhead Coalition seeks consensus and has been instrumental in bringing sometimes warring parties together. The group works closely with other Buckhead associations, including the Buckhead Business Association, merchants' groups, restaurant and bar owners, and the 44 neighborhood associations in the community.

THE COALITION TRIAD

The Buckhead Coalition works in three major areas: planning, marketing, and service to citizens. In 1994, in response to growth projections by

"THROUGH ORDERLY GROWTH, BUCKHEAD CAN MAINTAIN ITS SPECIAL QUALITY OF LIFE," SAYS SAM MASSELL, PRESIDENT OF BUCKHEAD COALITION, INC. AND FORMER MAYOR OF THE CITY OF ATLANTA (TOP).

BUCKHEAD COALITION, INC. GENERATES SEVERAL THOUSAND DOLLARS EACH YEAR FOR LOCAL NONPROFIT GROUPS, AND RECIPIENTS HAVE INCLUDED ATLANTA SPEECH SCHOOL, BUCKHEAD HOSPICE, BUCKHEAD YMCA, ATLANTA INTERNATIONAL SCHOOL, SHEPHERD CENTER, AND ATLANTA HISTORY CENTER. IN ADDITION, BUCKHEAD IS HOME TO SEVERAL ACADEMIC INSTITUTIONS (BOTTOM).

School, Shepherd Center, and Atlanta History Center. The organization disseminates news through the media on a regular basis, publishes the annual *Buckhead Guide Book*, and was a catalyst for the writing and publication of *Buckhead: A Place for All Time*, a history book on the area. Representing the Coalition and its concept, Massell speaks throughout metro Atlanta "to share our formula."

Another element, service to citizens, is perhaps the most unique aspect of Buckhead Coalition's efforts. The group has been described as a chamber of commerce, a visitors bureau, and a town hall. Says Massell, "We are some of all of these. We try to satisfy the requirements of our citizens, merchants, and businesspeople, whether by contacting the agency that can solve their problems, intervening on behalf of a neighborhood, or providing conveniences and amenities that enhance the quality of life."

The Buckhead Coalition's programs have ranged from underwriting the cost of bicycle racks and bike paths to providing free emergency street phones in the retail/entertainment area, the Village, in downtown Buckhead. The group backed the remaking of a park at a critical Buckhead gateway, complete with a sculpture, *The Storyteller*, a stylized buck telling stories to other animals. Another initiative, in partnership with a local hospital, was to make available for $350 a portable defibrillator—usually costing $4,000—to any building in Buckhead that houses more than 500 people. It was the first such communitywide project in the nation.

Recently, the Buckhead Coalition took a huge step in planning and spearheading the drive for the creation of a community improvement district (CID), a self-taxing commercial district in which residents and businesses vote to tax themselves for selected purposes. Among the possible uses of funds are road improvements, bus shuttles, traffic calming measures, parking facilities, and pedestrian and street amenities.

"Through orderly growth, Buckhead can maintain its special quality of life," says Massell.

city planners, the Coalition presented the Buckhead Blueprint, a long-range land-use plan and recommendations for balanced growth in the community covering an array of topics and concerns, from police protection and traffic patterns to schools and streetscapes. Many of those recommendations have been achieved.

In addition, the group generates several thousand dollars each year for local nonprofit groups, and recipients have included Atlanta Speech School, Buckhead Hospice, Buckhead YMCA, Atlanta International

A NAME TODAY RECOGNIZED THROUGHOUT METRO ATLANTA, BUCKHEAD IS A DISTINCTIVE COMMUNITY KNOWN FOR ITS BEAUTIFUL HOMES, STATELY HOUSES OF WORSHIP, EXCELLENT SCHOOLS, FINE RESTAURANTS, TRENDY NIGHTSPOTS, PRESTIGIOUS ART GALLERIES, LUXURY HOTELS, HIGH-RISE OFFICE BUILDINGS, AND UPSCALE SHOPPING CENTERS, SUCH AS PHIPPS PLAZA.

OFTEN REFERRED TO AS THE BEVERLY HILLS OF THE EAST, BUCKHEAD IS LOCATED WITHIN THE BOUNDARIES OF THE CITY OF ATLANTA AND ENCOMPASSES APPROXIMATELY 28 SQUARE MILES. MORE THAN 66,000 PEOPLE LIVE IN THE COMMUNITY, WHICH BOASTS THE HIGHEST PER CAPITA INCOME IN THE STATE.

I N THE VAST WORLD OF DOMESTIC AND INTERNATIONAL TRAVEL, THE amount of information that is processed every minute of every day is almost incomprehensible. Managing that information with unparalleled reliability and accuracy is Atlanta-based WORLDSPAN, one of the world's leading electronic commerce companies. ❑ Planning on booking a flight from Atlanta to New York's LaGuardia Airport?

CLOCKWISE FROM TOP RIGHT:
EXTENSIVE EXPERIENCE IN ELECTRONIC COMMERCE HAS MADE WORLDSPAN ONE OF THE TOP 10 DEVELOPMENT COMPANIES ON THE INTERNET AND A LEADING PROCESSOR OF INTERNET TRAVEL BOOKINGS. THE COMPANY'S WEB SITE IS LOCATED AT WWW.WORLDSPAN.COM.

WORLDSPAN IS COMMITTED TO SUPPORTING THE COMMUNITIES IN WHICH IT OPERATES.

WITH WORLD HEADQUARTERS IN ATLANTA, WORLDSPAN HAS OFFICES OR REPRESENTATION IN MORE THAN 60 COUNTRIES.

A travel agent using WORLDSPAN has the ability to instantly access all scheduled service, as well as nearly 160 fares available among the carriers flying that route. Consider the thousands of routes for travel inside the United States and internationally, and you quickly realize that WORLDSPAN must maintain up-to-date information for carriers worldwide and for literally millions of different airfares. WORLDSPAN is designed with the capacity and flexibility to meet the growing demands of today's travel industry, including the requirement for constant updating of schedules and fares.

Thanks to WORLDSPAN and its ability to manage comprehensive information every day, travel agents and corporate travel offices around the globe can effortlessly and accurately book all types of travel for their customers. WORLDSPAN presents extensive information on airlines, car rentals, hotels, cruises, rail services, tour operators, entertainment, local weather, and numerous other travel-related products and services. Working behind the scenes to capture and distribute the most current information, WORLDSPAN provides worldwide communications and electronic distribution of information for nearly 800 travel service providers.

With its world headquarters located in Atlanta and international headquarters in London, England, the company has offices or representation in some 60 countries. WORLDSPAN employs more than 3,100 people around the globe, with about 1,800 located in Atlanta. WORLDSPAN is Atlanta's third-largest computer service company and among the area's top 25 high-tech employers. Also, WORLDSPAN is one of Atlanta's top 20 privately held companies, according to the *Atlanta Business Chronicle*.

WORLDSPAN employees are committed to giving back to their communities. The company focuses on activities ranging from mentoring programs for local schools to the support of the Toys for Tots campaign. Other projects in which WORLDSPAN and its employees are actively involved include Habitat for Humanity, the Susan G. Komen Race for the Cure, and Food Harvester campaigns.

EXTENSIVE CAPABILITIES

WORLDSPAN delivers a wide array of capabilities for both major and regional airlines, and is a leading provider of mainframe and technical services to the airline industry. In the United States, for example, WORLDSPAN is among the largest processors of airline boardings. The company is owned by Atlanta-based Delta Air Lines, Northwest Airlines, and Trans World Airlines, giving WORLDSPAN more than 200 years of travel experience. In addition to providing services to its three airline owners, WORLDSPAN supplies a number of other airlines with various technology services, such as mainframe

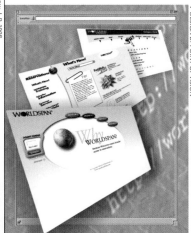

hosting, reservations and airport processing, and voice and data network communications.

Worldspan has also made an impact on the World Wide Web by supplying its database, expertise, and technologies to an increasing number of Internet-based, consumer-oriented travel information and booking sites. Today, Worldspan is one of the top 10 electronic commerce development companies on the Internet, and among the leading processors of Internet travel bookings. The company's Web site (www.worldspan.com) offers extensive information on Worldspan's products and services.

Worldspan's daily business involves a variety of impressive statistics. The company's database, for example, stores between 300 million and 600 million international and domestic airfares, a number that fluctuates according to the season, sales, and other marketing issues. Likewise, the average number of passenger travel records in the system is 17.2 million. To handle this much

information and more, the Atlanta-based data processing center has more than 3,200 gigabytes of disk storage capacity in tandem with a huge and complex mainframe infrastructure.

Committed to Customer Service

Perhaps the most telling statistic about the Worldspan data processing center is its unparalleled reliability and dependability. In spite of the massive amounts of information handled by the system, especially during peak periods, Worldspan maintains virtually 100 percent availability, 24 hours a day, seven days a week.

While Worldspan has always employed valuable technology tools for information distribution, the company has taken a leadership position in the development of software and systems to enhance its service offerings. One example is Worldspan Trip Manager^{SM}, an Internet-based self-booking tool. Trip Manager allows travelers to take travel planning into their own hands, while giving travel

agencies and travel managers the means to administer and enforce corporate travel policy and to realize significant cost savings.

Worldspan Go!^{SM} is another unique travel management tool. Go! facilitates comprehensive travel planning in one integrated system and enables travel agents to easily utilize information available on the Internet to check out a variety of topics of interest to customers, such as local weather conditions, State Department warnings, and maps. With Worldspan Go!, travel agencies can better serve their customers without learning or managing new technology.

Competing in the Global Marketplace

Increased globalization is significantly affecting the travel industry as airlines and travel-related companies merge and form strategic partnerships. Also, the nature of travel is changing as more tourism and business travel become international in scope.

Recognizing that change is implicit in this trend, Worldspan's global network provides the company with a strategic advantage in continuing to play a dominant role in this global environment.

Worldspan's success is rooted in the success of its customers. As the company continues to grow, its vision is to broaden its range of services, and to offer value-added products and programs for tomorrow's travelers. This philosophy will position Worldspan for continued excellence in what it knows best—the business of travel technology.

The North Highland Company

THE NORTH HIGHLAND COMPANY GETS INSIDE ITS CLIENTS' BUSINESS; IN fact, doing so is what the firm is all about. Founded in Atlanta in 1992, the fast-growing, independent management and technology consulting firm's goal is to help businesses run better. ❏ North Highland expects its clients to achieve enhanced revenues, better productivity, cost controls, higher quality, and keener competitiveness. "Basically, we want companies to perform better, faster, and cheaper," says David Peterson, founder and president. "We employ the latest technology where it has bottom-line benefits and we use business process improvements to create value."

To do so, North Highland provides a range of services, including business process management, information technology management, strategic planning, supply chain management, call center development, and data warehousing, along with manufacturing and distribution industry and health care industry services.

In Tune with the Client

One company served by North Highland, a $40 million business with distribution centers outside Atlanta, wanted to reduce its 11-week on-hand inventory to eight weeks through an adjustment of its computer systems. North Highland consultants were able to reduce inventory to four weeks, and inventory costs dropped from $6 million to about $3 million. Improvement came, however, through changes in procedures rather than in computer systems. "We helped the company by changing its thinking more than its systems," says Peterson.

For a Fortune 500 company based in Atlanta, North Highland performed a technology assessment that suggested a major overhaul to its customer system. "We were hired to serve as general contractor to replace hardware, software, processes, and procedures, and to handle change management," says Peterson. "We helped the client succeed in a complex technology area they could not have handled themselves."

North Highland assists large and medium-sized companies, and much of its work comes through referrals by satisfied clients. Among the firm's clients are the American Cancer Society, BellSouth Corporation, Chick-Fil-A, Harbinger Corporation, eShare Technologies, Shop'n Chek, and the State of Georgia.

Since its inception, North Highland has grown rapidly and consistently. In 1999, the firm was named by the *Atlanta Business Chronicle* as one of the top 20 fastest-growing private companies in the city. The company also landed a spot on *Inc.* magazine's prestigious Inc. 500 list. Additionally the company's president was named a finalist for the regional 1999 Ernst & Young Entrepreneur of the Year award.

Local Provider, National Presence

Though headquartered in Atlanta, North Highland currently has offices in Orlando and Nashville as well. Having local offices keeps travel demands to a minimum, allowing employees to participate in the communities in which they live. Limited travel also helps attract and keep talented employees. Other appealing features include the company's entrepreneurial spirit and the employee stock-ownership program. In fact, North Highland is 100 percent employee owned.

In 1999, North Highland effected its first merger with Renaissance Partners, Inc., a Marietta-based national customer support services leader that specializes in customer call center operations. The move allowed North Highland to assume a national presence in the field.

As it moves toward its next years of service, North Highland will continue to grow its core services while developing new strengths in the areas of call center services, E-commerce, customer relationship management, and knowledge management. And it will pursue its goal of making clients work better, faster, and cheaper.

FIVE OF THE NORTH HIGHLAND COMPANY'S CONSULTANTS DISCUSS A CLIENT MATTER. THEY RELY ON THEIR EXPERIENCE TO QUICKLY UNDERSTAND THEIR CLIENTS' NEEDS AND TO CREATE BUSINESS SOLUTIONS ADAPTABLE TO CLIENTS' OPERATING ENVIRONMENTS.

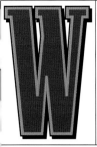

ELLSTAR HEALTH SYSTEM IS A LOCAL HEALTH SYSTEM WITH A NAME THAT reflects its mission: reaching for the stars to bring health and wellness to its communities. WellStar strives to be a comprehensive, neighborhood health care system that serves Cherokee, Cobb, Douglas, and Paulding counties in northwest Atlanta. ❑ WellStar is comprised of five of the area's oldest and strongest community hospitals—Cobb,

Douglas, Kennestone, Paulding, and Windy Hill—as well as WellStar Physicians Group, a group of more than 600 primary care providers, specialists, and advanced practitioners; medical centers; neighborhood health care centers; fitness facilities; home health services; hospice; senior living communities; and the WellStar Foundation. More than 8,000 employees and 700 area volunteers complement the full medical staff at each hospital.

CLOSE TO THE COMMUNITY

What sets WellStar apart is its close involvement with the community. "We are community owned and led, and are governed by local leaders who receive no compensation for their service," says WellStar CEO Thomas E. Hill. "Our goal is to put wellness within everyone's reach."

WellStar reaches out beyond its facilities with programs designed to promote wellness and safety at all stages of life, from prenatal to hospice care. Partnerships are frequent with local organizations that strive to bring the community quality care. For example, WellStar works with Safe Kids Coalition in

four counties to provide car seats, bike helmets, and smoke detectors to those in need. WellStar also partners with the local school systems and has provided school nurses in more than five school districts, in addition to supplying first aid supplies and comprehensive clinic manuals to 191 area schools.

Additionally, WellStar provides free or discounted health screenings, classes, and support groups for the community, including diabetes and prostrate screenings and pregnancy and arthritis self-help courses. Also, WellStar grants scholarship funds to help support the Kennesaw State University Nurse Practitioner Training Program. Many graduates stay in the community and work in WellStar facilities.

ADVANCED MEDICAL TECHNOLOGY

One of WellStar's newest facilities is the Jean and Mack Henderson Women's Center at Kennestone. "It is a state-of-the-art center that carries on our tradition of using the most advanced medical technology and combining it with very personal care,"

says Hill. This multigenerational center provides services for women at every stage of life. "It answers a tremendous need in this area," adds Hill. Among its three maternity units, WellStar delivers more than 9,000 babies annually.

Through WellStar's cancer program, one of the largest accredited comprehensive cancer programs in the Southeast, Well-Star Cobb and Kennestone hospitals are part of the nationwide Study of Tamoxifen and Raloxifene (STAR), one of the largest breast cancer prevention trials in history. WellStar's rehabilitation programs are among the highest rated in the country. And in early 1999, WellStar reached beyond its community by showing on the Internet a knee replacement surgery performed at WellStar Cobb Hospital by a member of WellStar's medical staff.

For the future, WellStar's mission is to exceed the expectations of the community by providing exceptional health care services dedicated to personal care, quality, and value. It believes new technology and old-fashioned caring are the keys to carrying out this mission.

FROM LEFT:
UNDER THE LEADERSHIP OF PRESIDENT ROBERT A. LIPSON, M.D. (LEFT), AND CEO THOMAS E. HILL, WELLSTAR STRIVES TO BE A COMPREHENSIVE, NEIGHBORHOOD HEALTH CARE SYSTEM THAT SERVES CHEROKEE, COBB, DOUGLAS, AND PAULDING COUNTIES IN NORTHWEST ATLANTA.

THE JEAN AND MACK HENDERSON WOMEN'S CENTER AT KENNESTONE IS A MULTIGENERATIONAL FACILITY FEATURING HEALTH CARE SERVICES AND PROGRAMS FOR WOMEN OF ALL AGES.

REGULAR HEALTH SCREENINGS FOR THE COMMUNITY REINFORCE WELLSTAR HEALTH SYSTEM'S COMMITMENT TO HEALTH AND WELLNESS.

Shorter College

SHORTER COLLEGE'S ROOTS ARE DEEP IN GEORGIA SOIL. FOUNDED IN 1873 in the town of Rome (about 60 miles northwest of Atlanta), Shorter has drawn students from all over Georgia since it opened its doors. In 1992, Shorter spread its roots farther from its traditional campus well into metro Atlanta. The college established the School of Professional Programs (SPP), designed to offer bachelor's and master's degree programs for working adult professionals.

THE WAVE OF THE FUTURE— NONTRADITIONAL STUDENTS

In a few short years, these professional programs, located in two metro county office complexes, have attracted 900 students, a number equal to the student body at the Rome campus. "We plan even greater growth for the future for both our Rome campus and our School of Professional Programs," says Shorter President Larry McSwain. "Shorter will continue its progress in attracting an ever brighter student body of about the same size in Rome, and will double the size of its School of Professional Programs."

Over the coming years, McSwain anticipates that SPP will add several more classroom sites and that the number of metro Atlanta students will reach 2,000. In addition, he says, "Shorter is planning much more collaboration with other institutions, both in the United States and overseas, and a greater focus on international learning."

The School of Professional Programs is peopled with nontraditional students—full-time working adults whose age, ethnic background, race, and religion mirror the diversity of Atlanta's population. Their shared goal to earn a degree while they continue to work gives them a commonality as well as a high degree of motivation. The minimum age for admittance into the program is 23, and the median age of these students is 35. A member of SPP's first graduating class in 1994 was in his 60s—an airline executive who was fulfilling a promise to his mother to finish college.

Women comprise about 70 percent of the students, and a large number of both men and women are middle managers in Atlanta's thriving corporate world. Because of the span of ages, diverse backgrounds, and life and work experiences, these students gain insights from each other that they might otherwise never encounter. And, adds McSwain, "This makes for some lively discussions in class."

IN THE REAL WORLD

SPP courses, offered only at night, are designed specifically for persons who have not completed their college education. Most students have some college hours and usually complete the Shorter program in about 22 months. Attendees take one class at a time, every five or six weeks. Taught by academically credentialed business profession-

FOUNDED IN 1873 IN THE TOWN OF ROME (ABOUT 60 MILES NORTHWEST OF ATLANTA), SHORTER HAS DRAWN STUDENTS FROM ALL OVER GEORGIA SINCE IT OPENED ITS DOORS.

als, the classes stress real-world relevancy of the subject matter. In fact, many students do their final major projects on topics or problems directly related to their workplaces.

One of the strong points of each program is that the class—generally 15 to 25 students—stays together from beginning to graduation. "This creates small groups that develop into intense teams for learning and application, and form incredibly strong support groups," comments McSwain. Says one 42-year-old student, who, besides working full-time, supports and nurtures a family and runs a household, "I don't think I could do this without the active support of my group. We call each other; we collaborate and commiserate. We all understand how hard it is to do this with all the other demands in our lives. And every one of us understands how important it is, too." This student will receive her bachelor of science degree in business administration and plans to continue in the Shorter School of Professional Programs to earn her master of business administration degree.

On the Hill

At Shorter College in Rome, the campus is in an idyllic setting atop Shorter Hill (or "the Hill," as it is called by students, college personnel, and townspeople), adjacent to an ancient

forest and overlooking the Coosa River and the city of Rome. Its expansive quadrangle is flanked by classic buildings of red brick and white columns, an architectural genre that is also reflected in the campus' new structures in an ongoing expansion program.

Founded originally as the Cherokee Baptist Female College, the present-day coeducational liberal arts college has won a reputation for academic excellence throughout the state and the Southeast. The school, which values its Christian heritage, offers a personal education and is, in McSwain's description, " an intimate, familial learning environment with considerable interaction between students and faculty."

Shorter's largest degree program is education. The school has also built an excellent natural sciences curriculum, and its pre-professional programs prepare students for rigorous graduate pursuits: Shorter boasts a 77 percent acceptance rate for its pre-med students, and 90 to 91 percent for pharmacy school and physical therapy school applicants. In addition, the college is strong in teaching communications arts and has an expanding business program.

The Sound of Music

Mention Shorter College in the world of music—especially voice, piano, organ, and church music—and the response is universal: excellence. The first Georgia school to be accredited by the National Association of Schools of Music, Shorter is known throughout the nation for the quality of its musical instruction and student accomplishment. The Shorter Chorale and Chorus perform nationwide and internationally, and have won worldwide distinction and invitations to perform. More than 80 percent of Shorter music graduates work in their field—surely adding a joyful noise to this world, according to McSwain. On the Hill, in metro Atlanta, and wherever the future may take Shorter College, he says, "Our job is to change people so they can change the world."

At Shorter College in Rome, the campus is in an idyllic setting atop Shorter Hill (or "The Hill,"as it is called by students, college personnel, and townspeople), adjacent to an ancient forest and overlooking the Coosa River and the city of Rome.

Internet Security Systems (ISS)

BY 2002, INTERNET COMMERCE IS EXPECTED TO REACH AS MUCH AS $3 trillion. As Web use and open computer networking spread rapidly around the globe, security breaches and network attacks escalate at the same speed. Viruses, worms, backdoor infiltration, industrial espionage, internal misuse, identity theft—the list of threats continues to expand. Enter Internet Security Systems

(ISS) to provide protection.

Founded in 1994, the Atlanta-based company has quickly taken the lead with its E-business risk and security management solutions. Its revenues and profits have skyrocketed, its growth has shot up 40 percent annually for the last few years, it has won numerous awards for its products, and it has captured 40 percent of market share in a relatively young industry that is growing rapidly.

A major global player in this market and one of the world's fastest-growing software companies, ISS has offices throughout the United States and international operations in Asia, Australia, Europe, and Latin America as well. Its customers include nearly all of the largest U.S. commercial banks, nine of the 10 largest telecommunications companies, more than 35 government agencies, firms in the Global 2000 and Fortune 1,000, and more than 3,000 organizations worldwide.

To protect computer networks from security threats, ISS pioneered a revolutionary technology with a scanning software that performs network vulnerability tests, detects security weaknesses, and provides a guide to eliminate those weaknesses.

THE TECHIE AND THE BUSINESSMAN

ISS founder and Chief Technology Officer Christopher Klaus is one of Atlanta's favorite self-made, Internet success stories. While a student at Georgia Institute of Technology in 1992, he developed ISS' security technology, and at the age of 21, founded his company to launch the first commercial version of the ISS Internet Scanner™. Klaus teamed up with Thomas Noonan, who was an experienced high-tech executive and who is now president and CEO of ISS.

Noonan, who has an engineering degree, worked for eight years in automated control systems, and Klaus is a security expert. They put their backgrounds together to create something entirely new. The two are business partners, close friends, and each other's toughest business critic.

In 1995, Klaus and Noonan were the company. Now they run an operation with more than 600 employees and customers around the world. "We are both having fun," remarks Noonan. The two promote the idea that creativity and business should be a labor of love. Says Klaus, "I want it to be fun around here, so that people will want to work for ISS and do their best."

Today, Klaus remains the technology guru and visionary, while Noonan is the businessman and strategist. "We are two very different people, but there is clearly a chemistry between us," says Noonan. "What solidifies our

CHRISTOPHER KLAUS, FOUNDER AND CHIEF TECHNOLOGY OFFICER, AND THOMAS NOONAN, PRESIDENT AND CHIEF EXECUTIVE OFFICER, COMBINED THEIR TALENTS IN 1992 AND FOUNDED INTERNET SECURITY SYSTEMS (ISS) IN ATLANTA IN 1994.

partnership is mutual trust and respect and our shared passion and belief in the need for and viability of our security products."

THE X-FORCE

ISS has carefully and consciously created an employee-friendly atmosphere, an environment with few rules and less structure than traditional corporate settings. It is a flat organization rather than a hierarchical one, and employees work as small teams with plenty of opportunity to use their own judgment. "People are the key to our leadership in the industry and our success," Noonan says, adding that ISS has a stringent recruiting program.

Klaus and Noonan have dubbed their tech teams the X-Force; these are the teams that develop new solutions for customers. "They are always pushing the limits," Noonan says, and they must be able to do their best work, even in a chaotic environment. High-tech

companies must move ever faster and must employ people who can innovate in the midst of this chaos.

The company offers a range of solutions in adaptive network security management, which includes security assessment; intrusion detection; and response software that addresses both types of security risks—vulnerabilities and threats.

AN OPEN PARTNERSHIP

A common problem for companies with technology networks comprised of products from multiple vendors is getting the systems to interface smoothly and effectively. In response to this situation, Internet Security Systems launched the Adaptive Network Security Alliance in 1998. The groundbreaking program has brought together more than 50 of the industry's leading infrastructure and application companies in an open, technology-focused initiative. The goal is to encourage the

development of effective standards in order to deliver interoperability between security products, security infrastructure, and network management systems. According to ISS, such interoperability enables a whole new level of effective security implementation and enforcement. The company was one of the first in the industry to open up its products to interoperate broadly with products of other companies.

As the Internet continues to expand, privacy is paramount to security. "Our mission is to be the trusted security adviser for our customers," says Noonan. ISS recognizes that it must maintain its focus to stay on track in a fast-paced market. "The Internet has forever changed the way we live, communicate, interact, and do business," he comments. What's more, what he perceives as the next version of the Internet will create even greater needs for security. Ahead lie boundless opportunities for ISS.

ISS' X-FORCE TEAMS DEVELOP NEW SOLUTIONS FOR CUSTOMERS. "THEY ARE ALWAYS PUSHING THE LIMITS," SAYS NOONAN, AND THEY MUST BE ABLE TO DO THEIR BEST WORK, EVEN IN A CHAOTIC ENVIRONMENT. HIGH-TECH COMPANIES MUST MOVE EVER FASTER AND MUST EMPLOY PEOPLE WHO CAN INNOVATE IN THE MIDST OF THIS CHAOS.

Marietta Conference Center & Resort

THE MARIETTA CONFERENCE CENTER & RESORT (MCCR) EVOKES A SENSE of the classic Old South: Flanked by lush, green lawns and bright flowers, a long, sweeping driveway leads to the imposing white, Greek Revival-style building situated atop one of the highest hills of Marietta's rolling terrain. ❏ The facility is designed to provide "living, leisure, and learning," says Chuck Ocheltree, senior vice

president, sales and marketing. "We are a resort, a country club, a local dining and events destination, and a conference center for meetings, serving regional and national corporations, as well as our community."

A SOUTHERN FLAVOR

The southern flavor of the Marietta Conference Center & Resort is evident in the richness of its wood, marble, art, and furnishings. Throughout the lobby, murals commissioned for the center depict the 1850s era, including scenes of young cadets from the Georgia Military Institute, which originally occupied the site.

Panoramic views of the rolling countryside, Kennesaw Mountain, and the Atlanta skyline greet guests from the columned Veranda, where fans hum lazily over wooden rocking chairs and iron filigree café tables. The lawn rolls away to an 18-hole championship golf course; constructed in 1915, it is one of the oldest in metro Atlanta.

Marietta Conference Center & Resort is within a short stroll of Marietta Square, the historic center of the town, which was founded in 1833. On the grounds of the resort is the fully restored, 1851 Brumby Home and Gardens, original home of Colonel Anoldus VanderHorst Brumby, superintendent of the Georgia Military Institute. Today, the home and gardens are popular for meetings, parties, weddings, and special events.

LIVING, LEISURE, AND LEARNING

With 20,000 square feet of meeting space and a business center, the 200-room resort is equipped with the latest, state-of-the-art audiovisual and electronic technology, and can accommodate up to 500 people. Most of the resort's conference business is corporate, including a number of Fortune 100 companies. The resort primarily serves clients in the Southeast, while a significant number also come from the Northeast and from national and international companies doing business in Atlanta. Technical groups, consulting firms, and training seminars are among the major users of the facility.

The resort hosts more than 750 conferences and meetings each year. The facilities and programs are designed to provide leisure and luxury to unwind—golf, tennis, swimming, a workout area with a sauna, an excellent meal, an evening at The Pub, or just rocking on the Veranda enjoying the view.

BUILT ON CORE VALUES

In 1990, the City of Marietta purchased the 132 acres the Marietta Conference Center &

Resort is now built on to protect the green space and parklike grounds. The preservation and restoration of Brumby Home and Gardens, listed on the National Register of Historic Places, were also part of the decision to buy the land. The Marietta Country Club had previously occupied the site until relocating to Kennesaw, Georgia.

The city believed that the construction of the Marietta Conference Center & Resort would enhance the historical significance of the property, as well as provide a place for the community to gather. The City of Marietta then sought out a qualified management and development company who shared the same vision—Sentry Hospitality Ltd.

"The Marietta Conference Center & Resort is our flagship property," says Mark Magarity, president and CEO of Sentry Hospitality Ltd. "It is a showpiece for the City of Marietta and for Sentry, not only in beauty, service, accommodations, and amenities, but also in operations and financial performance." Business has been strong since the property opened, and Sentry's track record of revenue and profit is substantially above industry standards.

Magarity founded Sentry in 1993, and the company quickly positioned itself as a leader in its segment of the conference, resort, and hotel industry. Based in Manhattan, the company develops and

manages upscale conference centers and conference resorts throughout the United States.

Magarity attributes Sentry's success to its commitment to a set of core values: "Our company is built upon a foundation of conducting business with honesty, integrity, and responsibility. Although markets, technology, and managerial trends change, this foundation should always remain constant, solid, and fixed."

One of the features of Sentry properties is its excellent service, evidenced by a 96 percent guest satisfaction level. "We try to employ people who really care about service," notes William H. Jackson, general manager of Marietta Conference Center & Resort and executive vice president of Sentry Hospitality. All employees must successfully complete a comprehensive program at Sentry Hospitality University, the conference center industry's only college-style training program. Developed by Sentry, the university offers courses that focus on service, exceeding guest expectations, company values, problem solving, and leadership. There are also advanced courses in specific areas of conference center and resort service, operations, and management.

FOR THE COMMUNITY

While business conferences comprise some 80 percent of its market, the Marietta

Conference Center & Resort is very much a part of the community. The resort's management has formed a 16-person Community Focus Council of local leaders to provide community input.

A majority of the city's civic groups hold their meetings at the resort, and it is a favorite spot for special occasions and events, hosting more than 120 weddings each year. Sunday Brunch draws a capacity crowd, and the resort's restaurant, Hamilton's has be-come a popular location for Marietta residents. As the destination of choice for families greeting wedding guests or Fortune 100 companies welcoming seminar participants, the Marietta Conference Center & Resort is certain to continue its tradition of excellence well into the new millennium.

BRUMBY HOME AND GARDENS, LISTED ON THE NATIONAL REGISTER OF HISTORIC PLACES, WAS RESTORED TO ITS ORIGINAL SPLENDOR IN MAY 1997. THE ANTEBELLUM HOME AND THREE-ACRE GARDENS PROVIDE AN ELEGANT SETTING FOR WEDDINGS, RECEPTIONS, SOCIAL FUNCTIONS, AND CORPORATE AFFAIRS (TOP LEFT AND RIGHT).

THE MARIETTA CONFERENCE CENTER & RESORT IS THE ONLY RESORT IN THE ATLANTA AREA THAT OFFERS GUESTS GOLF PRIVILEGES OUTSIDE THEIR DOORSTEP (BOTTOM LEFT).

THE SANFORD CONFERENCE ROOM IS ONE OF TWO 1,700-SQUARE-FOOT CONFERENCE ROOMS COMPRISING THE 22,462-SQUARE-FOOT CONFERENCE CENTER (BOTTOM RIGHT).

The Leader Publishing Group, Inc.

**I**T'S ONE THING TO PLUNGE INTO THE VOLATILE WORLD OF MAGAZINE publishing. It's quite another to close the first year of business with many accolades, high readership, all start-up loans paid off, and a profit. But for Gina Wright, who founded The Leader Publishing Group, Inc. (LPGI) in Atlanta in 1997, it's what she expected—and a little more. ❏ "We have a conservative business plan. If you bite

off more than you can chew, you get in trouble," says Wright, who wears the hats of president, CEO, and publisher, and keeps a close eye on sales. "We were certain that we wanted to show a profit. Also, we felt we had a good product that would fill a void in the market. Atlanta is a vibrant, growing business center, yet it did not have a comprehensive, well-written, visually appealing business magazine."

A SUCCESSFUL VENTURE

Wright began the company's flagship product, *Business to Business*, in April 1997. B2B, as it is dubbed locally, is a slick, four-color product replete with features, columns, and quick reads, and focuses on business in metropolitan Atlanta. Since the magazine's inception, each issue has been comfortably thick with a mix of editorial content and advertising. In her April/May 1998 "Publisher's Hello," Wright reported, "In our first year, we have exceeded all expectations. *Business to Business* has outpaced every single industry standard in terms of growth, and is larger in circulation and pagination than any other local business magazine." The magazine began in 1997 as a quarterly publication, became bimonthly

after one year, and is now published monthly, quite a feat for a fledgling publication.

In 1999, the Magazine Association of Georgia recognized the magazine's success by awarding B2B three silver awards and one bronze at the annual GAMMA Awards lunch.

RECOGNIZING A NICHE

Even with B2B's early success, Wright seized another opportunity. "During the course of its first year of publication, *Business to Business* defined itself for the 40-plus age market," notes Wright. But this meant that a vast number of small, independent, and entrepreneurial businesses in the area still weren't being served by her company. To embrace this market niche, LPGI created *Catalyst*, introduced as a bimonthly business magazine in September 1999, for the under-40, up-and-coming crowd. It's an easy, fast read with cutting-edge graphics, stimulating images, and short, lively articles.

To add balance to LPGI business early on, Wright established a custom publishing division. Focused on creating in-house maga-

GINA WRIGHT IS CEO OF THE LEADER PUBLISHING GROUP, INC. AND PUBLISHER OF *Business to Business* AND *Catalyst* MAGAZINES (TOP).

REALIZING THE FOREMOST CHALLENGE FACING ANY NEW MAGAZINE IS TO BUILD AWARENESS, WRIGHT PURSUED BRANDING OPPORTUNITIES, NEGOTIATING AN AGREEMENT WITH METRO ATLANTA RAPID TRANSIT AUTHORITY (MARTA) AND TDI TO FEATURE *Business to Business* MAGAZINE ON 75 OF ATLANTA'S TRANSIT BUSES, GENERATING HUNDREDS OF THOUSANDS OF IMPRESSIONS. THIS SUCCESSFUL CAMPAIGN CREATED A BUZZ, AND TODAY, THE MAGAZINE IS OFTEN IDENTIFIED BY READERS AS "THE ONE YOU'VE SEEN ON THE BACK OF THE BUSES" (BOTTOM).

A T L A N T A

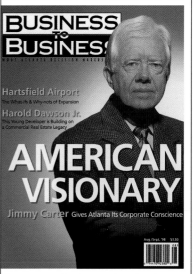

Atlantan who knew the city, its business, and its character.

A Ton of Fun

"The magazine business is a ton of fun," says Wright, adding that it is the one place she believes her interests in art, words, and sales come together. "But publishing is a business," she emphasizes, "one that takes careful planning and careful execution. It also takes considerable sales presence in the community and a quality product." Selective in hiring only those who share her passion, Wright believes in surrounding herself with the most knowledgeable people.

Wright is a highly visible and effective company representative throughout the business community. Behind the scenes, she spends time and resources on research and development, always listening to her magazine audiences and responding to reader demands. "*Catalyst* is really a brainchild of the Atlanta business community," Wright comments. "We didn't give them a magazine and say, 'This is what you should read.' We asked, 'What do you want to read?' "

And from all indications, what Atlanta businesspeople want to read are LPGI's growing business publications. Backed by a combination of passion and fiscal practicality, The Leader Publishing Group, Inc. continues to develop into a major player on the local media scene.

zines for corporations, this segment is expected to grow substantially in the coming years. Wright also anticipates adding to LPGI's stable of business magazines through acquisition or start-up, and she plans to continue targeting niche markets. "We will not try to be all things to all people, and we don't care to go where others have gone before," explains Wright.

Pursuing a Passion

For Wright, publishing magazines is a passion. A journalism major who attended college on scholarship, she veered into sales as vice president of a medium-sized publishing company in Raleigh. But Wright had her eye on Atlanta. "It's a city of opportunity," she says, and her own market research proved her hunch that there was plenty of demand for a business magazine in the metropolitan area.

After resigning from her sales job, Wright moved to the Big Peach in time to devote countless hours of volunteer work during the 1996 Summer Olympic Games. At the same time, she developed a business plan, hoping to form a joint venture that would bring her passion to fruition. When the dream did not materialize, Wright accepted a position as head of a custom publishing operation in Atlanta. But the compromise left her too far from her dream.

Wright eventually resigned and began to polish her business plan, putting together numbers and financials while searching for investors and an editor who would grow with the company. And after sifting through 80 responses to her ad for an editor, she chose Tim Darnell, an experienced writer and editor, and a native

Platinum Television Group

I**N THE MARKETPLACE, TIMING CAN BE EVERYTHING. WALTER BURTON AND** Doug Scott appear to have perfect timing in the founding and development of their young company, Platinum Television Group. Conceived in 1997, the media services company produces national television shows, corporate training programs, demo products, and other fee-based media services. It has expanded rapidly into Internet services, instructional videos on CD-ROM, direct mail, and publication marketing.

As Burton, who serves as vice president of the company, says, "Virtually anything a client can conceive, Platinum Television can achieve." The approach has paid off. The company's revenues have skyrocketed more than 250 percent each quarter since it was established.

NICHE MARKETING

Currently, the company's largest segment of business is its highly successful consumer educational TV programming under the umbrella of its American Lifestyle Series. *New Home Journal*, *This Week in Real Estate*, and *The Auto Report* are half-hour shows that have achieved almost 100 percent penetration in the top 200 markets across the country via cable, local networks, and major affiliates in all 50 states and in much of Canada.

The shows are designed on a national platform that includes advice and tips from high-profile experts in the field. On the local level, *New Home Journal* and *This Week in Real Estate* feature a wealth of information on communities, mortgage rates, property taxes, pricing, building specifications, how to negotiate buying or

selling a home, and moving companies, while *The Auto Report* instructs car buyers on issues such as dealerships, guarantees, and rebates. Notes Scott, Platinum Television Group president, "We have found a niche to bring the local consumer up to date with the latest information in his or her city, town, and community."

Real estate and auto sales are truly local. While there may be broad national trends, each market has its own personality and its own needs. Platinum Television identifies those local trends and incorporates them into each show. In addition, sponsors and advertisers include large national companies as well as local advertisers. In preparing the show for each market, the company's in-house TV crews cover each city and town thoroughly.

Platinum has developed its own full-time staff in production, editing, research, script writing, and other necessary areas. "We do our own shooting and editing," says Burton, adding that the company does work with local agencies for acting talent. "By keeping our production in-house, we have control over quality, and we think it is important to maintain our reputation in the eyes of viewers, show participants, and advertisers."

Those advertisers are vital to the company's TV success. Platinum advertises its shows extensively in national and local media, usually with four-color ads. According to Scott, the company has more than $7.5 million in advertising in the printed press, primarily through trade-out arrangements. The exposure in print advertising and to TV viewers continues to draw big-name experts to participate in the shows.

Hotlanta

Although the city's summer weather would be reason enough, the inspiration for Atlanta's nickname, Hotlanta, was the tremendous growth on all fronts; the metro area is among the top five hottest markets in the country for real estate and new home buying. The area follows the national trend of rapid growth in housing for active adults and baby boomers, and in the particular demands of those segments. But the metro area also has its own distinctive requirements in the styles of homes, amenities, decor, and lifestyle considerations.

For example, in building or buying a new home in Atlanta, buyers look first at communities that suit their lifestyles, then they choose a builder—a reverse of previous trends. Platinum Television Group's Atlanta shows reflect this local trend. "We present in-depth footage of a range of communities to give viewers a flavor of what each locale is all about," explains Burton. "Atlanta has a great variety of different communities—more than in many other markets. We make sure that our Atlanta shows highlight this distinction. This attention to each market is what makes us stand out amid the huge number of TV productions out there."

A Vast, New Market

Scott and Burton, who first met when they both worked for the same TV production company, are broadening Platinum's reach beyond television channels to the Internet. In a joint venture with Quatro Systems, Inc., an established Internet development company in Philadelphia, the duo has formed icasttv.com to bring television programming to the Internet. Launched in September 1999, icasttv.com is targeting various industries, beginning with new home construction. "Essentially, through the Internet, we are offering 24-hour programming to an audience that is absolutely exploding in numbers," says Scott. "We are marrying the cutting edge of technology in the Internet with educational programming to link consumers to industries vital to their everyday lives."

Both Scott and Burton are in their early thirties, and as children of the technological age, their vision is unlimited. "The incredible possibilities of the Internet have barely been touched, especially as it becomes interactive through the consumer's television," says Burton. "We believe that we are on the leading edge of this huge, new market." The future promises exciting opportunities for the rapidly growing company.

Doug Scott (left) and Walter Burton appear to have perfect timing in the founding and development of their young company, Platinum Television Group. Conceived in 1997, the media services company produces national television shows, corporate training programs, demo products, and other fee-based media services.

Sheraton Atlanta Hotel

THE SHERATON FLAG FLIES PROUDLY OVER THE SHERATON ATLANTA HOTEL AT Courtland Street and International Boulevard in downtown Atlanta. Well known and highly respected in hospitality worldwide, the Sheraton name now graces the city's first convention hotel, which is rich in history. ❏ The Sheraton Atlanta Hotel emphasizes personal service, comfort, and amenities, along with functionality in the latest business

and communications capabilities for corporate, leisure, and convention guests. The hotel is designed to accommodate groups ranging from small, one-day corporate meetings to conventions of 500 people or more.

Recently, the 765-room hotel underwent a comprehensive, $31 million renovation with decor that has added a sense of the whimsical to its boutique feel. A dramatically tented entry leads into the hotel's corridors, which feature an undulating wave motif; bright, contemporary colors; and lively restaurants—all of which have added a festive and modernist air to the property. Large windows and walkways between the hotel's two towers bring the liveliness of the city's bustle to view.

One of the Sheraton Atlanta Hotel's most enchanting features is its indoor swimming pool, set among lush, tropical gardens laced with intricate, wrought-iron grillwork. The setting resembles the private courtyards of historic Savannah. General Manager Michael Deighton notes that guests find the pool area an oasis

in the middle of the city, and it is a popular spot for group functions for conventioneers, politicians from the nearby Georgia capital area, and Atlantans' weddings, receptions, and special events.

A ROLE IN ATLANTA HISTORY

A part of much of Atlanta's history, the Sheraton Atlanta Hotel stands on the site of the original cabin built in 1833 by Hardy Ivy, the city's first permanent settler, before Atlanta was founded as a terminus in 1837. Opening in 1965 as the city's first convention hotel, it was constructed with meeting and banquet rooms and exhibit space designed to accommodate conventions. In fact, the hotel played a leading role in developing Atlanta's convention industry, which has grown to become a $4 billion business for the metro area.

At a time when controversy over segregation was fervid, the Atlanta Sheraton was one of the first hotels in the city to practice integration for both its guests and its employees. Through the years, it has been a frequent meeting place for elected officials when the Georgia legislature is in session. A few of the many well-known guests of the hotel have been Jimmy Carter,

Gerald Ford, Ronald Reagan, Dick Van Dyke, Mr. T, Hank Aaron, and Muhammad Ali.

No one has personally welcomed more of the hotel's guests than James R. Jones, or Mr. J., as he is better known. A doorman extraordinaire, he was the hotel's first hourly employee when the property opened in 1965 under Marriott ownership, and he continues to greet guests with an abundance of southern hospitality and charm. "Mr. J. represents what the Sheraton Atlanta Hotel offers everyone who walks through its doors—warmth, friendliness, and true southern hospitality," says Deighton, "He is an outstanding ambassador."

The hotel was acquired jointly in 1998 by Angelo, Gordon & Co., a New York-based investment firm, and Amerimar Enterprises, Inc., a Philadelphia-based company that specializes in the redevelopment of urban commercial properties. "We are proud of this hotel's role in Atlanta's history," says Deighton. "It is fitting that this important landmark and participant in Atlanta's well-known hospitality industry is now a Sheraton. We plan to continue to enhance its reputation and its role."

THE SHERATON ATLANTA HOTEL EMPHASIZES PERSONAL SERVICE, COMFORT, AND AMENITIES, ALONG WITH FUNCTIONALITY IN THE LATEST BUSINESS AND COMMUNICATIONS CAPABILITIES FOR CORPORATE, LEISURE, AND CONVENTION GUESTS (TOP).

GENERAL MANAGER MICHAEL DEIGHTON NOTES THAT ONE OF THE MOST ENCHANTING FEATURES OF THE SHERATON ATLANTA IS ITS INDOOR SWIMMING POOL, A POPULAR SPOT FOR GROUP FUNCTIONS FOR CONVENTIONEERS, POLITICIANS FROM THE NEARBY GEORGIA CAPITAL AREA, AND ATLANTANS' WEDDINGS, RECEPTIONS, AND SPECIAL EVENTS (BOTTOM).

Towery Publishing, Inc.

EGINNING AS A SMALL PUBLISHER OF LOCAL NEWSPAPERS IN THE 1930S, Towery Publishing, Inc. today produces a wide range of community-oriented materials, including books (Urban Tapestry Series), business directories, magazines, and Internet publications. Building on its long heritage of excellence, the company has become global in scope, with cities from San Diego to Sydney represented by Towery products. In all its endeavors, this Memphis-based company strives to be synonymous with service, utility, and quality.

A DIVERSITY OF COMMUNITY-BASED PRODUCTS

Over the years, Towery has become the largest producer of published materials for North American chambers of commerce. From membership directories that enhance business-to-business communication to visitor and relocation guides tailored to reflect the unique qualities of the communities they cover, the company's chamber-oriented materials offer comprehensive information on dozens of topics, including housing, education, leisure activities, health care, and local government.

In 1998, the company acquired Cincinnati-based Target Marketing, an established provider of detailed city street maps to more than 300 chambers of commerce throughout the United States and Canada. Now a division of Towery, Target offers full-color maps that include local landmarks and points of interest, such as parks, shopping centers, golf courses, schools, industrial parks, city and county limits, subdivision names, public buildings, and even block numbers on most streets.

In 1990, Towery launched the Urban Tapestry Series, an award-winning collection of oversized, hardbound photojournals detailing the people, history, culture, environment, and commerce of various metropolitan areas. These coffee-table books highlight a community through three basic elements: an introductory essay by a noted local individual; an exquisite collection of four-color photographs; and profiles of the companies and organizations that animate the area's business life.

To date, more than 80 Urban Tapestry Series editions have been published in cities around the world, from New York to Vancouver to Sydney. Authors of the books' introductory essays include former U.S. President Gerald Ford (Grand Rapids), former Alberta Premier Peter Lougheed (Calgary), CBS anchor Dan Rather (Austin), ABC anchor Hugh Downs (Phoenix), best-selling mystery author Robert B. Parker (Boston), American Movie Classics host Nick Clooney (Cincinnati), Senator Richard Lugar (Indianapolis), and Challenger Center founder June Scobee Rodgers (Chattanooga).

To maintain hands-on quality in all of its periodicals and books, Towery has long used the latest production methods available. The company was the first production environment in the United States to combine desktop publishing with color separations and image scanning to produce finished film suitable for burning plates for four-color printing. Today, Towery relies on state-of-the-art digital prepress services to produce more than 8,000 pages each year, containing well over 30,000 high-quality color images.

AN INTERNET PIONEER

By combining its longstanding expertise in community-oriented published materials

TOWERY PUBLISHING PRESIDENT AND CEO J. ROBERT TOWERY HAS EXPANDED THE BUSINESS HIS PARENTS STARTED IN THE 1930S TO INCLUDE A GROWING ARRAY OF TRADITIONAL AND ELECTRONIC PUBLISHED MATERIALS, AS WELL AS INTERNET AND MULTIMEDIA SERVICES, THAT ARE MARKETED LOCALLY, NATION-ALLY, AND INTERNATIONALLY.

ATLANTA

with advanced production capabilities, a global sales force, and extensive data management expertise, Towery has emerged as a significant provider of Internet-based city information. In keeping with its overall focus on community resources, the company's Internet efforts represent a natural step in the evolution of the business.

The primary product lines within the Internet division are the introCity(TM) sites. Towery's introCity sites introduce newcomers, visitors, and long-time residents to every facet of a particular community, while simultaneously placing the local chamber of commerce at the forefront of the city's Internet activity. The sites include newcomer information, calendars, photos, citywide business listings with everything from nightlife to shopping to family fun, and online maps pinpointing the exact location of businesses, schools, attractions, and much more.

DECADES OF PUBLISHING EXPERTISE

In 1972, current President and CEO J. Robert Towery succeeded his parents in managing the printing and publishing business they had founded nearly four decades earlier. Soon thereafter, he expanded the scope of the company's published materials to include *Memphis* magazine and other successful regional and national publications. In 1985, after selling its locally focused assets, Towery began the trajectory on which it continues today, creating community-oriented materials that are often produced in conjunction with chambers of commerce and other business organizations.

Despite the decades of change, Towery himself follows a long-standing family philosophy of unmatched service and unflinching quality. That approach extends throughout the entire organization to include more than 130 employees at the Memphis headquarters, another 60 located in Northern Kentucky outside Cincinnati, and more than 50 sales, marketing, and editorial staff traveling to and working in a growing list of client cities. All of its products, and more information about the company, are featured on the Internet at www.towery.com.

In summing up his company's steady growth, Towery restates the essential formula that has driven the business since its first pages were published: "The creative energies of our staff drive us toward innovation and invention. Our people make the highest possible demands on themselves, so I know that our future is secure if the ingredients for success remain a focus on service and quality."

TOWERY PUBLISHING WAS THE FIRST PRODUCTION ENVIRONMENT IN THE UNITED STATES TO COMBINE DESKTOP PUBLISHING WITH COLOR SEPARATIONS AND IMAGE SCANNING TO PRODUCE FINISHED FILM SUITABLE FOR BURNING PLATES FOR FOUR-COLOR PRINTING. TODAY, THE COMPANY'S STATE-OF-THE-ART NETWORK OF MACINTOSH AND WINDOWS WORKSTATIONS ALLOWS IT TO PRODUCE MORE THAN 8,000 PAGES EACH YEAR, CONTAINING WELL OVER 30,000 HIGH-QUALITY COLOR IMAGES (TOP).

THE TOWERY FAMILY'S PUBLISHING ROOTS CAN BE TRACED TO 1935, WHEN R.W. TOWERY (FAR LEFT) BEGAN PRODUCING A SERIES OF COMMUNITY HISTORIES IN TENNESSEE, MISSISSIPPI, AND TEXAS. THROUGHOUT THE COMPANY'S HISTORY, THE FOUNDING FAMILY HAS CONSISTENTLY EXHIBITED A COMMITMENT TO CLARITY, PRECISION, INNOVATION, AND VISION (BOTTOM).

Photographers

ALLSPORT was founded the moment freelance photographer Tony Duffy captured the now-famous picture of Bob Beamon breaking the world long- jump record at the Mexico City Olympics in 1968. Originally head-quartered in London, Allsport has expanded to include offices in New York and Los Angeles. Its pictures have appeared in every major publication in the world, and the best of its portfolio has been displayed at elite photographic exhibitions at the Royal Photographic Society and the Olympic Museum in Lausanne.

© BUD LEE

PATRICIA L. BLOOD, a graduate of the University of Alabama, has returned to school as a photography instructor for the Spruill Center for the Arts. A self-proclaimed military brat, Blood now resides in Decatur, Georgia, as the owner and operator of Spittin' Image Studios.

CRAIG BROMLEY, a native Atlantan, participated in apprenticeships in London, Paris, and Milan early in his photography career. Upon his return to Atlanta in 1987, he established Craig Bromley Photography, specializing in corporate portraits. His clients include Arthur Andersen; Canine Assistance, Referral & Education (CARE); Coca-Cola; and the Woodruff Arts Center, but Bromley is best known for his timeless black-and-white images of Atlanta's street corners.

ORAIEN E. CATLEDGE has had work published in *Atlanta Magazine* and the *Tulanian*, and has been featured on NBC's Bob Dotson's *American Dream*. With an advanced degree in social work from Tulane University, Catledge worked for the American Foundation for the Blind for more than 20 years. Currently, he is developing some 50,000 negatives taken in an old Atlanta mill community known as Cabbagetown.

HAROLD DANIELS—with clients including BellSouth, IBM, Equitable, and Emory University—has built an impressive résumé, focusing in advertising and corporate photography. A native of Bells, Tennessee, Daniels now lives in Atlanta, where he is an employee of Ice House Studio.

DAVID ALAN DOBBS has been published in *National Geographic Explorer, U.S. News & World Report*, and *Life*, as well as in Towery Publishing's *Celebrating a Triangle Millennium*. He won an ADDY in 1981 for photography, as well as a first-place award in the 1980 International Association of Business Communicators contest.

NEVILLE DUFFIELD, a native of London, England, now makes his home in Cincinnati. With a master's degree in mechanical engineering, He is a General Electric engineer in the aircraft engine division.

THOMAS S. ENGLAND's parents were educators for the Department of Defense and, as a result, he grew up in many different parts of the world. While obtaining a degree in film from Northwestern University, England began his career as a photographer, concentrating on the antiwar and civil rights movements of the 1960s. He became a staff photographer for Pioneer Press in Chicago, and, in 1974, was assigned to photograph for *People Magazine*. England has been freelancing since then, covering national and international news events, personalities, and locations for such publications as *Time, Newsweek*, the *New York Times*, and *National Geographic*.

CHARLENE FARIS, a native of Fleming County, Kentucky, is the owner and operator of Charlene Faris Photos. Specializing in travel, historic, and inspirational photography, Faris has won numerous awards, including several from the National League of American Pen Women art shows. She was a 1994 Pulitzer Prize nominee for wedding photos of Lyle Lovett and Julia Roberts, which have now been published in more than 20 nations. Faris also completed an art project for the Hoosier Salon with a grant from the Indiana Arts Commission and the National Endowment for the Arts. Faris' images have appeared in several Towery publications, including *Orlando: The City Beautiful, St. Louis: For the Record*, and *San Antonio: A Cultural Tapestry*.

CHRIS HAMILTON is the owner and operator of Atlanta-based Chris Hamilton Photography. Hamilton specializes in sports, travel, time-lapse, and architectural photography, and his clients include the Atlanta Braves, Kodak Professional, and Coca-Cola. He was named the official photographer for the 1996 Atlanta Paralympic Games and the 2000 Olympic Games in Sydney.

RUSSELL HOLLOWAY, a native of Columbus, Georgia, has called Atlanta home since 1974. The owner of Holloway Photography, he specializes in advertising and corporate photography.

BILLY HOWARD is a commercial and documentary photographer with an emphasis on health, education, and social themes. Howard is the author of *Epitaphs for the Living: Words and Images in the Time of AIDS; Portrait of Spirit: One Story at a Time*—images and interviews of people with disabilities with a forward by Christopher Reeve—and *Godzilla-vs-Cancer: Images and Imaginings of Children with Cancer*. His work has been exhibited internationally, and is in the permanent collections of the Library of Congress, the High Museum of Art, the Savannah College of Art and Design, and the Carter Center.

CAROLINE JOE, the owner and operator of CJOESHOOT, is a transplanted Atlantan from Houston. Specializing in advertising, corporate, and editorial portraiture, Joe has photographed for Nestlé, Rolls-Royce, McCall's, MCA Records, and *Seventeen*.

STAN KAADY moved to the Atlanta area in 1998 from Portland, Oregon. With a bachelor of fine arts degree in editorial and corporate photography from Rochester Institute of Technology, Kaady now claims MCI, the American Heart Association,

Atlanta Medical Center, and Microsoft as clients.

ROD KAYE produces sports, editorial, and fine art photography out of his Marietta-based Rod Kaye Photography Studio. After leaving his northeastern Pennsylvania home in 1984, Kaye made his way south to study at the Portfolio Center in Atlanta. Today, he shoots for *Sports Illustrated* and *American Photo*.

LAURA NOEL, a native Atlantan, received a bachelor of arts degree in public policy studies from Duke University in 1988. After jobs in New York City and South Carolina, Noel returned home to freelance from her Atlanta-based Noel Photography Studio. Her work has been seen in *Life*, *People Magazine*, *Time*, *USA Today*, and the *Washington Post*.

PHOTOPHILE, established in San Diego in 1967, is owned and operated by Nancy Likins-Masten. An internationally known stock photography agency, the company houses more than a million color images, and represents more than 90 contributing local and international photographers. Subjects include extensive coverage of the West Coast, business/industry, people/lifestyles, health/medicine, travel, scenics, wildlife, and adventure sports, plus 200 additional categories.

EDGAR SOLIS moved to the Atlanta area from San Juan, Puerto Rico, in the summer of 1991. Specializing in commercial, architecture, and editorial photography, he now owns and operates Edgar Solis Photography.

MARILYN SURIANI completed a bachelor of arts degree in sociology and psychology from Georgia Southern University before studying documentary photography at the Portfolio Center in Atlanta. She has received grants from the City of Atlanta Bureau of Cultural Affairs and the Georgia Council for the Arts, and is currently on commission for a permanent exhibit at Hartsfield International Airport.

KIMBERLY A. WAGES spent six months in Atlanta studying dance with the Atlanta Ballet before moving to the city permanently to continue work at Georgia State University. As a lab manager at Spitfire Imaging, Wages works with many of Atlanta's top corporations and public relations-design firms.

STEVE WARBLE, director of orchestras for the Barrington, Illinois, public school system, developed an interest in photography as a result of his numerous journeys to national parks and wilderness areas throughout the United States and Canada. He is the owner of the Elgin, Illinois-based Mountain Magic Photography, which specializes in stock photo sales and decor photography. Warble's work has been featured in dozens of magazines, calendars, and environmental displays, as well as in Towery Publishing's *Toronto Tapestry*.

MARK W. WOLFE, a retired engineer, now focuses his time and energy on photography. As the owner and operator of Mark Wolfe Photography at Moving Spirits Studios, he specializes in black-and-white documentary photography.

GREGORY WILLIAMS, a lifelong resident of Savannah, graduated from the Savannah Technical Institute and has studied under renowned nature photographer John Earl. In his freelance career, Williams specializes in landscape, unique architecture, and abstract photography, and many of his images are used in chamber of commerce guides across the nation. He has won several regional Sierra Club photo contests and, in 1996, mounted an exhibit titled *Savannah and the Georgia Coast*. His images have also appeared in Towery Publishing's *Jacksonville: Reflections of Excellence*, *Greater Phoenix: The Desert in Bloom*, and *Seattle: Pacific Gem*.

ZUMA PRESS is an international assignment and stock photo agency formed in 1993 by a group of photographers and award-winning journalists. Its unique photography files encompass a range of subjects, from the military to politicians, business leaders, movie stars, medical and scientific trends, and circus performers. Zuma is also committed to developing human interest features and in-depth documentary photo-essays for immediate syndication.

Additional photographers and organizations that contributed to *Atlanta: The Right Kind of Courage* include the Atlanta History Center, Folio, Inc., and International Stock.

© BUD LEE

LIBRARY OF CONGRESS CATALOGING-IN-PUBLICATION DATA

Carter, Jimmy, 1924-
  Atlanta : the right kind of courage / Jimmy Carter ; art direction by Jil Foutch.
      p.   cm. — (Urban tapestry series)
  Includes index.
    ISBN 1-881096-73-4 (alk. paper)
      1. Atlanta (Ga.)—Civilization.   2. Atlanta (Ga.)—Pictorial works.   3. Atlanta
  (Ga.)—History—20th century.   4. Carter, Jimmy, 1924—Childhood and youth.   I. Title.   II.
    Series.
  F294.A84 C38 2000
  975.8'231—dc21   00-026022

© BUD LEE

Try our Famous TRAIN WRECK !

Towery Publishing, Inc.
The Towery Building
1835 Union Avenue
Memphis, TN 38104
WWW.TOWERY.COM

PUBLISHER: J. Robert Towery EXECUTIVE PUBLISHER: Jenny McDowell NATIONAL SALES MANAGER: Stephen Hung MARKETING DIRECTOR: Carol Culpepper PROJECT DIRECTORS: Mary Beth Cardoni, Henry Hintermeister, Joy Murray, Robert Philips, Lizabeth Simmons EXECUTIVE EDITOR: David B. Dawson MANAGING EDITOR: Lynn Conlee SENIOR EDITOR: Carlisle Hacker EDITOR/PROFILE MANAGER: Stephen M. Deusner EDITORS: Jay Adkins, Brian Johnston, Ginny Reeves, Sunni Thompson ASSISTANT EDITOR: Rebecca Green EDITORIAL ASSISTANT: Andrew Harlow PROFILE WRITER: Judith Schonbak CAPTION WRITER: Sunni Thompson CREATIVE DIRECTOR: Brian Groppe PHOTOGRAPHY EDITOR: Jonathan Postal PHOTOGRAPHIC CONSULTANT: Monika Nikore PROFILE DESIGNERS: Laurie Beck, Melissa Ellis, Laura Higley, Ann Ward PRODUCTION MANAGER: Brenda Pattat PHOTOGRAPHY COORDINATOR: Robin Lankford PRODUCTION ASSISTANTS: Robert Barnett, Loretta Lane DIGITAL COLOR SUPERVISOR: Darin Ipema DIGITAL COLOR TECHNICIANS: Eric Friedl, Brent Salazar, Mark Svetz PRINT COORDINATOR: Beverly Timmons

Index of Profiles

© BUD LEE